THE UNOFFICIAL GHIBLI PARK COOKBOOK

50+ Delightful Recipes Inspired by the WHIMSICAL THEME PARK and MOVIES from Your Favorite JAPANESE ANIMATION STUDIO

ANDY CHENG

ULYSSES PRESS

Published by:
ULYSSES PRESS
PO Box 3440
Berkeley, CA 94703
www.ulyssespress.com

ISBN: 978-1-64604-7-253
Library of Congress Control Number: 2024934568

Printed in China
10 9 8 7 6 5 4 3 2 1

Acquisitions editor: Shelona Belfon
Managing editor: Claire Chun
Editor: Phyllis Elving
Proofreader: Barbara Schultz
Front cover and interior design: Winnie Liu
Photographs: © Andy Cheng except page 9 red bean paste lovelypeace/shutterstock.com; pages 9, 15 focaccia © Zagorulko Inka/shutterstock.com; pages 9, 16 rice © MSPT/shutterstock.com; pages 9, 24 Shiratama dango © sasazawa/shutterstock.com; page 22 kanten © New Africa/shutterstock.com

CONTENTS

Chapter 3

DESSERTS AND SWEET TREATS 119

INTRODUCTION

WHAT'S IN THIS BOOK

The Unofficial Ghibli Park Cookbook is my debut cookbook, with recipes that allow you to prepare iconic foods from Ghibli Park and popular Studio Ghibli films. As a qualified epidemiologist, I've turned to cooking as my stress reliever and break away from the public health realm. This opportunity to share wonderful food inspired by Studio Ghibli's iconic stories combines two of my greatest loves: art and cooking. It has also taught me to appreciate a range of foods from various cultures, including Japanese, Italian, and British dishes. I hope this cookbook will inspire you to go into the kitchen and enjoy a bit of magic in cooking.

THE MAGIC OF STUDIO GHIBLI

Studio Ghibli, the acclaimed animation film studio, was founded in 1985 in Tokyo by Hayao Miyazaki, Isao Takahata, and Toshio Suzuki. Studio Ghibli is widely known for its exceptional filmmaking and artistry, for which it has won critical and popular praise. Studio Ghibli has captivated moviegoers with fantastic stories of magic, adventure, friendship, and family. The Walt Disney Company and the Tokuma Shoten Publishing Company, which controls Studio Ghibli, formed a partnership in 1996, making Disney the sole international distributor of the world-renowned animated films.

One successful film produced by Studio Ghibli animation was *Princess Mononoke*, released in Japan in 1997 and in the United States two years later. The 2002 film *Spirited Away* was named the best-animated feature at the Hong Kong Film Awards and received The Golden Bear, the top prize at the Berlin International Film Festival.

Food is a critical feature in Studio Ghibli productions, as every film showcases scenes of the characters cooking, eating, and sharing the most mouthwatering animated food. These scenes have symbolic meaning in line with the storylines. In *Spirited Away*, for example, the

character Chihiro is shown eating a red bean bao, symbolizing comfort and the sense of belonging that accompanies going back home. These cooking scenes make the animated worlds of Studio Ghibli come to life, closely connecting food with family and emotion. I hope this cookbook brings that same bit of magic to the real world for you!

THE WHIMSICAL WORLD OF STUDIO GHIBLI PARKS

Studio Ghibli Park, located in Nagoya, Japan, is a magical destination for fans of the beloved animation studio. Opened in 2022, the park immerses visitors in the enchanting worlds of Ghibli classics such as *My Neighbor Totoro*, *Spirited Away*, and *Howl's Moving Castle*. Nestled within the larger Expo 2005 Aichi Commemorative Park, this park features life-size replicas of iconic buildings, lush gardens, and interactive exhibits that bring the studio's fantastical landscapes to life. A visit to Studio Ghibli Park offers a unique opportunity to step inside the imagination of Hayao Miyazaki and experience the whimsical charm and profound beauty that define Ghibli films.

The park also offers a delightful culinary experience, with themed restaurants that transport guests into the heart of Ghibli's enchanting worlds. At the Flying OVEN, inspired by *Kiki's Delivery Service*, visitors can enjoy delectable dishes conjured up in the film. Alternatively, after exploring the Grand Warehouse—filled with Studio Ghibli's most famed film sets—they can head to the Transcontinental Flight Café for indulgent sandwiches, focaccia pizzas, and more. Each dining spot within the park not only provides delicious food but also extends the immersive Ghibli experience, allowing guests to savor the magic of these beloved stories with every bite.

HOW TO USE THIS BOOK

This cookbook includes classic Japanese dishes, foods inspired by Studio Ghibli Park, and a few recipes from the magical films themselves. While it mainly features Japanese cuisine, there are recipes inspired by international foods showcased in the park and in the films. Ingredient substitutions are suggested, too. Just like animation, cooking is an art, and I encourage you to add your own spin to the dishes!

It's worth noting that each cafe within the park utilizes seasonal menus, which means that some items might appear during certain times of year while others might not. The ingredients used in dishes may also vary depending on the time of year. So if you wonder why a dish from this book isn't on the menu at Ghibli Park, or doesn't look exactly the same, the recipe is authentic to the park experience but reflects a menu item for a particular season.

ESSENTIAL INGREDIENTS

Throughout Japanese cuisine, there is a host of ingredients that play a pivotal role in many classic dishes. Many will be used in the recipes throughout this book, so it's good to get familiar with those ingredients!

DASHI: Dashi is a fundamental Japanese broth, known for its delicate yet complex umami flavor and aroma. It is traditionally made by simmering kombu (dried kelp) and katsuobushi (dried bonito flakes). Other variations include dried shiitake mushrooms and small fish. Dashi is the basis for many Japanese classics, such as miso soup, broth, and sauces, as well as a few of the recipes in this book.

If you want to make your own, soak a ½-ounce piece of kombu in 4 cups of water in a medium saucepan for 30 minutes. Then, slowly bring to a boil over medium-low heat. Using a ladle, skim any foam that comes to the top and discard. When the water just comes to a boil, turn off the heat, remove the kombu, and add in ½ ounce of bonito flakes. Cover with a lid and leave for 15 minutes. Then strain the dashi through a strainer lined with a kitchen towel over a bowl.

Nowadays, you can find dashi packs in Asian supermarkets, which are much more convenient and just as delicious!

SAKE: Sake, known as Japanese rice wine, is a traditional alcoholic drink made by fermenting polished rice. While enjoyed as a beverage, it is also used in many Japanese culinary recipes, adding a unique depth of flavor with its sweetness and umami notes.

MIRIN: Mirin is a sweetened Japanese rice wine. While it has a lower alcohol content than sake, it has a higher sugar content, giving a distinct sweetness, depth, and complexity to many dishes, sauces, and marinades.

SOY SAUCE: One of Japan's staple condiments, soy sauce is known for its rich, salty, and umami flavor. Made from fermenting soybeans with wheat, salt, and water, you'll find soy sauce being used in countless dishes. Light soy sauce has a more delicate flavor, enhancing the natural flavors of other ingredients. On the other hand, dark soy sauce adds a more deep and robust flavor while adding a darker color to the dish.

MISO PASTE: Miso is made from fermented soybeans, salt, and koji (a mold culture used in fermentation) and comes in various types and colors. White miso has a mild and slightly sweet taste, while red miso is richer, pungent, and has a bolder flavor profile. Miso is known for its deep umami, adding a distinct flavor to sauces, broths, and marinades.

BASIC RECIPES

The first chapter of this book will teach you how to make the bases for many of the upcoming recipes, such as ciabatta, focaccia, Japanese rice, and more. As some of these recipes may be time consuming and advanced, please note that store-bought versions of these bases will work just fine!

Chapter 1

BASIC RECIPES

CIABATTA

Who doesn't love ciabatta? This Italian bread is airy and fluffy on the inside, with a delightful crisp on the outside. While it does take a long time to make, your patience will be rewarded with the first delicious bite!

Makes: 8 to 10 small ciabatta rolls | Prep time: 5 hours |
Fermenting time: 12 to 24 hours | Cook time: 20 minutes

INGREDIENTS

Poolish
1⅛ cups (150 grams) bread flour

¼ teaspoon active dry yeast

5 ounces (10 tablespoons) water, at 105°F to 110°F

Ciabatta
poolish (above)

1 cup water at 105°F to 110°F

1½ tablespoons kosher salt

1½ tablespoons extra-virgin olive oil

3 cups bread flour

SPECIAL EQUIPMENT
stand mixer

1. Start by making the poolish. In a large bowl, use a rubber spatula to combine the 1⅛ cups bread flour and the yeast. Slowly stir in the 10 tablespoons water, using a large spoon to mix. Make sure there are no dry clumps of flour left, but don't overwork. Cover with plastic wrap and refrigerate for 12 to 24 hours.

2. Take out the poolish, which will have increased in size, developed a beerlike aroma, and become stretchy. Gently mix in 1 cup water, which will help release the mixture from the sides of the bowl. Add in the salt, olive oil, and 3 cups bread flour. Gently mix using a rubber spatula until well combined, with no dry patches of flour. Cover with plastic wrap and let rest for 30 minutes at room temperature.

3. After 30 minutes, transfer the dough onto a flour-dusted work surface. The dough should be very wet—but be patient with it. With wet hands, pick up the dough and slap it onto the work surface. In the same motion, pull the closest side slightly toward you and fold the dough over itself. The dough will be very sticky, but persevere! Repeat this process for 3 minutes. The dough will gradually become more elastic but still be quite wet. Clean the work surface every so often.

4. Transfer the dough to a greased bowl, cover with plastic wrap, and let rest for 45 minutes at room temperature.

5. Fill a large bowl with room-temperature water so you are able to submerge your hand. Dip your preferred hand into the water, then pull up the dough, stretch the dough edge, and fold it over on itself. Turn the bowl, again dip your hand in the water, pull up the edge of the dough, and fold it over itself. Repeat until you've worked around the entire dough edge. Place the dough back in the greased bowl, cover with plastic wrap, and let sit for 45 minutes. Repeat this process 3 more times (for a total of 4 times). Be gentle with the dough; it will slowly become more and more manageable.

6. Dust your work surface liberally with flour. Tip the bowl upside down over the work surface and let the dough fall out. Cut it into your desired sizes. To shape, take the left side of one piece and fold it a third of the way back over the dough. Repeat with the other side. Fold over 1 to 2 inches of the tops and bottoms. There should now be a seam on top.

7. Cover the dough pieces on the work surface with a large bowl or other container and let sit for 30 minutes. In the meantime, preheat your oven to 425°F, with a baking tray inside.

8. After 30 minutes, liberally dust flour onto parchment paper and on the top of the dough. Gently transfer the dough onto the parchment paper using a bench scraper if you have one. Slide the paper and dough onto a baking tray and then onto the tray in the oven. Using a spray bottle filled with water, immediately spray water around the inside of the oven.

9. Place the ciabatta into the oven and bake for 20 minutes. The baking time will depend on the size of your ciabatta and the strength of your oven. When the ciabatta is baked all the way through, it should have a light golden-brown color and sound hollow when tapped from underneath. Remove from the oven and let cool on a wire rack.

10. Use your ciabatta in your favorite sandwich recipes, such as the Tandoori Chicken Sandwich (page 79) or Saucy Spaghetti Sandwich (page 87).

FOCACCIA

This focaccia recipe is the basis for several other dishes in this book. While it takes a while to make, you will reap the rewards with the fluffiest and most delicious focaccia you'll ever taste!

Serves: 8 to 10 | Prep time: 20 minutes |
Fermentation time: 48 hours | Cook time: 35 to 40 minutes

INGREDIENTS
4 cups bread flour

½ cup wheat flour

1¾ cups water, at 105°F to 110°F

1 (¼-ounce) packet active dry yeast

pinch of sugar

1½ tablespoons salt

2½ tablespoons extra-virgin olive oil, plus more for the baking tray and dough surface

SPECIAL EQUIPMENT
stand mixer with dough hook

1. Place the measured ingredients in separate containers.

2. In the bowl of a stand mixer, mix together the bread and wheat flours.

3. In a separate small bowl, combine the water, yeast, and a pinch of sugar. Mix thoroughly with a fork and set aside at room temperature for 5 minutes to let the yeast activate. When ready, the mixture should be frothing at the top.

4. Using the dough hook on the stand mixer at medium-low speed, gradually add the yeasty water to the flour mixture. When the dough is starting to come together, add the salt and 2½ tablespoons olive oil and mix for another 10 minutes. By then the dough should have fully come together but still be quite wet.

5. Tip the dough onto an unfloured work surface, then pick it up and throw it back down. Fold the bottom back on itself, then pick the dough back up by the folded edges and repeat the process several times, until the dough has become slightly smoother and less sticky.

6. Coat the inside of a deep container with olive oil and place the dough inside. Cover with a lid or plastic wrap and refrigerate for 48 hours.

7. When the dough is ready, coat a 9 x 13-inch baking tray with olive oil and then tip the dough onto the tray, breaking as few bubbles as possible. Using your hands, gently spread the dough to the pan edges—but don't worry if it doesn't go all the way. Set another tray on top and let sit at room temperature for 1 hour. In the meantime, preheat your oven to 450°F.

8. There should now be lots of bubbles on the dough surface. You can leave them or remove them, as you wish. Add a generous amount of olive oil using a spoon and use the tips of all of your fingers to make small indents across the dough.

9. At this point you can add toppings, as called for in some of the following recipes. If you are baking without toppings, sprinkle on a generous amount of kosher salt.

10. Place in the oven and bake for 35 to 40 minutes, or until golden brown on top. Then remove and let cool on a wire rack for an hour. Slice into portions to serve.

NOTES

- Rest the focaccia for 2 days in the refrigerator to create an airy texture on the inside and a crunch on the outside. If this is too long, rest the dough at least 12 hours.

- For Step 7, if the dough feels a little tough, spread it out as much as you can, cover with another tray for 10 minutes, and then try spreading it out again.

- The baking time will vary from oven to oven, so keep an eye on the focaccia as it bakes. Turn the temperature up or down as needed.

Perfect
JAPANESE RICE

Rice is the basis of many Japanese dishes, but cooking it properly can be daunting, especially if you don't have a rice cooker. With this foolproof recipe, though, you'll be a master in no time!

Serves: 4 | Prep time: 40 minutes |
Cook time: 30 to 70 minutes, depending on the method used

INGREDIENTS

1½ cups uncooked Japanese short-grain rice

1⅔ cups water, at room temperature

Stovetop method
heavy pot

Rice Cooker Method
rice cooker cup
rice paddle
rice cooker

WASHING THE RICE

1. Add your rice to a medium bowl and add cold water until the rice is just submerged. Use one hand to hold the bowl in place and the other to wash the rice in circular motions for 10 seconds. The water should turn cloudy. Tip the rice out into a strainer to discard the water, making sure not to lose any of the rice.

2. Place the rice back into the bowl and repeat the process until the water remains clear. This should take about 3 to 5 washes.

STOVETOP METHOD

1. After washing your rice, transfer it to a large heavy pot. Add the 1⅔ cups water, close the lid, and let soak for 30 minutes.

2. Remove the lid and bring to a boil on the stovetop over medium heat. Boil for about 5 minutes, or until the bubbles become larger.

3. Mix with a rubber spatula and spread the rice so it is flat. Reduce the heat to as low as possible, place the lid back on the pot, and cook for another 10 minutes. The cooking time will vary depending on the type of pot you are using; a heavy pot will help spread the heat more evenly than a regular saucepan.

4. After 10 minutes, turn off the heat and leave the rice covered to steam for another 10 minutes. Then gently mix and fluff your rice before serving.

RICE COOKER METHOD

1. After washing your rice, add it to the rice cooker pot.

2. Add cold water to the rice cooker pot, level with the number 3 marking on the side of the rice cooker; add or remove water as needed. Place the pot in the cooker and close the lid.

3. Let soak for 30 minutes, then start the rice cooker. Depending on the rice cooker, it will take a further 50 to 70 minutes to cook the rice.

4. The rice cooker will beep or make a melodic noise once the rice has finished cooking. Immediately open the cooker and use a rice paddle to gently mix and fluff the rice. Then close the lid and let steam for 10 minutes before serving.

5. When using the stovetop method, resist the urge to lift the pan lid while the rice is cooking. The steam will escape and ruin the cooking process. It may take a few tries to perfect the cooking time for your stove and pan.

6. When you buy a bag of Japanese rice, it typically comes with a rice cup, which helps with measuring. One rice cup equates to ½ a regular cup in measurement.

NOTES

🍄 Cooking rice in a pot on the stovetop can be tricky. A rice cooker does away with all that stress, letting you make perfect rice every time.

SANDWICH ROLL

This roll is so versatile that you can use it for all sorts of recipes. Whether you eat it as a sandwich, toasted, or just by itself, you'll never want to buy bread from the supermarket again!

Makes: 6 to 8 sandwich rolls | Prep time: 20 minutes | Rising time: 1 hour 20 minutes | Cook time: 20 to 30 minutes

INGREDIENTS

1½ cups warm water (105°F to 110°F)

1 (¼-ounce) packet active dry yeast

1 tablespoon honey

2 tablespoons whole milk (105°F to 110°F)

4 cups bread flour

1½ tablespoons sugar

1 teaspoon salt

4 tablespoons unsalted cold butter, cubed

1. In a small bowl, use a spoon to mix the warm water with the yeast, honey, and milk. Let sit for 5 to 10 minutes.

2. In the bowl of a stand mixer, combine the bread flour and sugar. Over low speed, slowly add the warm water mixture and beat for 5 minutes. Increase to medium speed and add the salt. Then add a couple of cubes of the butter and beat until it is fully incorporated into the dough. Repeat for the rest of the butter.

3. Roll the dough out into a tight ball, cover with greased plastic wrap (so the dough won't stick when you remove the wrap), and place inside a greased bowl. Let sit at room temperature for 1 hour.

4. The dough should now be doubled in size. Hit the dough with your hand or a utensil to knock out some of the air, then scrape it onto a floured work surface. Divide it into 6 pieces, or more if you want smaller rolls. Roll each piece into a ball and then shape it into a cylinder, starting from the center and working out to create tapered ends.

5. Place the rolls on a baking tray lined with parchment paper. Loosely cover with a damp towel and let rise for 30 minutes at room temperature.

6. Using a razor or sharp knife, score the length of the dough pieces at a 45-degree angle. Preheat the oven to 400°F.

7. Bring a small, ovenproof pan of water to a boil on the stovetop. Once the water is boiling, place the bread in the oven and set the pan of water on the rack below it. Bake the rolls for 10 minutes; the water will help steam them.

8. After 10 minutes, remove the pan of water and bake the bread for another 20 minutes, or until golden brown. Then transfer the pan to a wire rack and let cool to room temperature.

NOTES

- If the yeast and water mixture doesn't froth after 5 to 10 minutes, the yeast is dead and cannot be used.
- If you make smaller rolls, the baking time will change, so keep an eye out while they are in the oven!

Essential
DESSERT RECIPES

The following dessert recipes are key for some of the dishes in this book. Some ingredients may be hard to find, but head to your local Asian or Japanese supermarket. They should be available there!

KANTEN (AGAR JELLY)

Makes: 6 to 8 servings | Prep time: 5 minutes | Cooling time: 30 minutes

INGREDIENTS
2 cups water
2 teaspoons agar powder
2 tablespoons sugar

1. Add the water and the agar powder to a small saucepan and bring to a boil over low heat. Once the agar powder is blended in, stir in the sugar.

2. Rinse an 8-inch-square baking pan with cold water. Add the kanten mix to the baking dish and let sit in the fridge uncovered for 30 minutes.

ANKO (SWEETENED RED BEAN PASTE)

Makes: 18 to 20 ounces | Prep time: 5 minutes |
Cook time: 45 minutes | Cooling time: 40 minutes

INGREDIENTS

1¼ cups (200 grams) uncooked red (azuki) beans

¾ cup sugar

½ teaspoon kosher salt, or more as needed

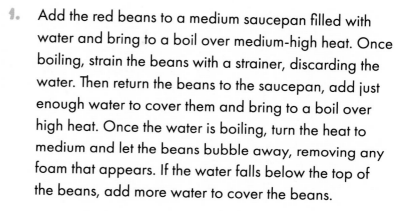

1. Add the red beans to a medium saucepan filled with water and bring to a boil over medium-high heat. Once boiling, strain the beans with a strainer, discarding the water. Then return the beans to the saucepan, add just enough water to cover them and bring to a boil over high heat. Once the water is boiling, turn the heat to medium and let the beans bubble away, removing any foam that appears. If the water falls below the top of the beans, add more water to cover the beans.

2. To check if the beans are cooked, pick one up with a rubber spatula and press it between your thumb and index finger. If you can easily break it without using any force, it's ready. In total, this process should take around 30 to 45 minutes.

3. Drain the beans using a strainer. Then add the sugar and salt, and mix thoroughly. Use a potato masher to crush some of the beans; you want some to be whole, some mashed. Then set aside to cool for 40 minutes. The beans should harden as they cool.

4. After 40 minutes, check the taste. Mash more beans and add more salt and a splash of water to loosen the mixture according to your personal liking. Transfer to a bowl, cover with plastic wrap, and refrigerate until needed. Anko can be stored for 3 to 5 days in the refrigerator.

SHIRATAMA DANGO (MOCHI BALLS)

Makes: 16 | Prep time: 10 minutes | Cook time: 5 minutes

INGREDIENTS

4 ounces shiratama flour
(sweet rice flour)

⅓ cup plus 1 tablespoon
cold water

1. Using a rubber spatula, mix the shiratama flour with the all of the water until it all comes together.

2. Portion the mixture into bite-size balls, then press the center of each ball lightly to flatten it slightly.

3. Bring a pot of water to a boil and add the shiratama dango balls. When they start floating, boil for 1 minute longer.

4. Remove from the boiling water and place in ice water to cool.

5. Keep submerged in cold water and use within 30 minutes after they are made otherwise they will become hard. If so, you reheat in some boiling water until soft.

Chapter 2
SAVORY DELIGHTS

Warm-Your-Heart
NABEYAKI UDON

Nabeyaki udon is a quick and simple wintertime classic in Japan. What better way to warm up than with thick and chewy noodles in a deep, umami-packed dashi broth, along with various vegetables and chicken pieces? Not to mention that this can be made in a single pot, known as a donabe or Japanese clay pot! Sit down in front of a roaring fire and enjoy this comforting noodle dish. Did you know that director Hayao Miyazaki of Studio Ghibli likes to top his ramen with spinach? That's what inspired the use of spinach in this recipe!

Serves: 1 | Prep time: 20 minutes | Cook time: 10 minutes

INGREDIENTS

2 slices carrot, peeled

2 stems spinach

2-inch piece Japanese leek (negi) or green onion

2 fresh shiitake mushrooms

2 ounces raw skinless chicken thigh

2¼ cups dashi (page 7)

1 tablespoon mirin

1 tablespoon sake (Japanese rice wine)

2 tablespoons soy sauce

1 teaspoon kosher sea salt

1 (7.3-ounce) pack precooked udon noodles

3 (¼-inch) kamaboko slices (processed Japanese fish cake)

1 medium egg

shichimi spice

1. Cut the carrot into ¼-inch-thick slices. If you have a star-shaped cutter, cut each slice into a star shape.

2. Remove the roots and cut the spinach into 2-inch pieces Slice the leek diagonally into 3-inch pieces. Cut the kamoboko into 3-inch slices.

3. Using a sharp knife, cut the stems off the shiitake mushrooms and then cut a flower shape on the mushroom tops. To do this, make 2 V-shaped slices facing each other. Rotate and repeat, then repeat 2 more times to create a flower shape.

4. Cut the chicken thigh into bite-size pieces.

5. Add your dashi, mirin, and sake to a donabe (Japanese clay pot) or a saucepan and bring to a boil over medium-high heat. Once boiling, turn the heat to low and stir in the soy sauce, sea salt, chicken thigh pieces, shiitake mushrooms, and carrot pieces. Cook for 5 minutes.

6. Add the preboiled udon noodles. Then add the kamoboko slices, spinach, and Japanese leek along the outer edge of the pan. Crack the egg on top. Cover with a lid and boil until the egg white is cooked through but the yolk is still runny.

7. Serve in the donabe pot or a bowl, topped with shichimi spice.

NOTES

🍄 For extra flavor, add the leftover shiitake mushroom scraps to the dashi mix.

🍄 Bringing the dashi, sake, and mirin mix to a boil will help burn off the alcohol from the sake.

🍄 If you use dried udon noodles rather than precooked ones, boil until about 70 percent cooked, then drain and rinse with cold water.

Classic
YAKI IMO

Yaki Imo is simply a baked sweet potato that is a classic Japanese dish. During the winter, small food vans roam the streets playing the song "Ishi Yaki Imo." The song can be heard throughout the area, so people quickly put on their coats and run to get their yaki imo.

"Ishi" means stones, as yaki imo are traditionally baked in a stone oven. The result is a sweet, fluffy, hot sweet potato that will make you forget the cold and warm you up on any winter day. Baking slowly intensifies the sweetness of the potato, which becomes so light and tender that it is sometimes even used as a dessert!

You can easily re-create the classic yaki imo at home with an ordinary oven, so let's get baking!

Serves: 4 | Prep time: 5 minutes | Cook time: 1 hour 20 minutes

INGREDIENTS
4 large sweet potatoes

1. Preheat the oven to 325°F.

2. Using a fork or skewer, poke holes around each sweet potato.

3. Bake in the oven for 1 hour and 20 minutes, or until tender. You can check by poking a potato with a fork.

4. Traditionally, yaki imo is enjoyed as is, but adding a pinch of flaky kosher sea salt will make a delicious balance of sweet and savory.

NOTES

- Using a fork to poke holes in the sweet potatoes will help let out some of the steam while cooking and keep them from exploding in the oven.

- You can wrap the sweet potatoes in foil or bake them as is. Wrapping them in foil will make them very moist and tender; without foil, the sweetness increases as the water inside evaporates.

- The skin of the sweet potatoes is full of nutrients, so you can definitely eat it!

- You can keep yaki imo in the fridge for 3 days after baking or freeze it for up to a month and then reheat in the oven.

Hiroshima
OKONOMIYAKI

This Hiroshima okonomiyaki is a variation of the classic Osaka-style okonomiyaki, or Japanese pancake dish. While Osaka-style mixes cabbage, flour, and egg into a batter that's fried like a pancake, Hiroshima-style layers the ingredients and adds yakisoba noodles and a fried egg. It's all topped with a special okonomi sauce, Kewpie mayonnaise, dried seaweed, and pickled ginger.

Hiroshima okonomiyaki is the perfect party food to share with friends and family. As you read through the recipe, all the ingredients and the flipping and turning can seem daunting, so I recommend reading through the notes on page 34 before you start! "Okonomi" in Japanese means "as you like," so feel free to add any ingredients you want! Popular choices aside from pork are squid and prawns.

Serves: 1 or 2 | Prep time: 40 minutes | Cook time: 15 minutes

INGREDIENTS
Batter
½ cup water
½ teaspoon salt
1 teaspoon mirin
2 ounces (½ cup) cake flour
or all-purpose flour
4 ounces cabbage
1 green onion
3 tablespoons bonito flakes
1 tablespoon tempura
scraps (pre-packaged)

1. In a medium bowl, combine ½ cup water, ½ teaspoon salt, and the mirin. Slowly stir in the cake flour, then cover and refrigerate for 30 minutes.

2. In the meantime, slice the cabbage and green onion into thin slices. If the bonito flakes are large, place them in a small bowl and use your fingertips to break them into small pieces.

3. Heat a medium nonstick skillet on the stovetop over medium heat and add 1 teaspoon of neutral-flavored cooking oil. Take the batter out of the refrigerator and stir. Then ladle about half of the batter into the heated skillet and spread to a size just slightly smaller than your serving plate.

1½ ounces fresh bean sprouts

3 thin slices raw pork belly

Kosher salt

5 ounces yakisoba noodles, preboiled

1 medium egg

1 large green onion

water

neutral-flavored cooking oil

Toppings

okonomiyaki sauce (see notes on page 34)

Kewpie mayonnaise

dried green seaweed (aonori)

pickled ginger (beni shouga)

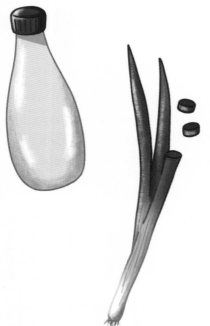

4. Sprinkle the bonito flakes onto the batter. Then add the cabbage and green onion pieces, tempura scraps, and bean sprouts on top.

5. Carefully lay on the pork belly pieces to cover the other ingredients, making sure the pieces don't overlap. Sprinkle on some salt and 2 tablespoons of the batter, to help bind the ingredients together. Cook for around 2 to 3 minutes.

6. When the "crepe" has cooked through, use a pair of spatulas to flip it over. Use a spatula to bring any loose ingredients back into the okonomiyaki, pressing down gently to make the top even.

7. In the meantime, heat a second nonstick frying pan over medium-high heat. Fry the yakisoba noodles in the pan, adding a tablespoon of water to help loosen them. Then mix in 2 tablespoons okonomiyaki sauce. Arrange the noodles in a circular shape the same size as the okonomiyaki.

8. When the bottom side of the okonomiyaki (with the pork) is golden brown and cooked through, use a pair of spatulas to transfer the okonomiyaki onto the noodles. Wipe the empty pan clean, add 1 tablespoon oil, and crack in the egg. Spread out the egg to try to make it the same size as the okonomiyaki, and sprinkle with salt. Before the egg has cooked through, transfer the okonomiyaki, crepe side up on top of it and cook for 1 minute.

9. Use the spatulas to flip the okonomiyaki one last time so the egg is on top. Transfer it onto a serving plate and top with the okonomiyaki sauce, spreading it with a spoon. Drizzle on Kewpie mayonnaise, then create streaks by using a wooden skewer or the tip of a knife to make lines across the mayonnaise. Top with dried green seaweed (aonori), pickled ginger, and the green onion pieces.

NOTES

- I recommend placing all the ingredients in separate small bowls to keep them organized, as there will be a lot going on while you're cooking. All the flipping and turning can be daunting, but don't worry! You can push all the ingredients to the center to bind them back together.

- Make sure to use medium heat, and take your time. That way you can assemble the ingredients carefully without burning anything.

- It looks like a lot of cabbage and bean sprouts are used in this recipe, but they will shrink when cooked.

- Customize your okonomiyaki to your liking with as much sauce, aonori, pickled ginger, and green onions as you want!

- You can find okonomiyaki sauce in your local Asian supermarket. You can also easily make it at home by combining 3 tablespoons of Worcestershire sauce, 1 tablespoon of ketchup, 2 teaspoons of oyster sauce and 1 teaspoon of sugar.

Miso Rice Soup
(MISO ZOUSUI)

Zousui is a comforting Japanese rice soup made with a dashi broth and various vegetables. Packed with nutrients, it's the perfect dish when you're feeling under the weather, want to warm up from the cold, or just want a quick and delicious meal! You can easily make it at home or out camping under the starry night sky as you seek out the help of a forest spirit.

Serves: 4 | Prep time: 10 minutes | Cook time: 20 minutes

INGREDIENTS

5 to 8 stalks nira (Chinese garlic chives) or green onions

1 pound Japanese short-grain rice, cooked

4 cups dashi (page 7)

3 tablespoons red miso, or to taste

1 tablespoon soy sauce

kosher salt, to taste

1. Cut the nira into 2-inch pieces and set aside.

2. Place the cooked rice and 2½ cups of the dashi in a medium saucepan. Bring to a boil over medium heat, stirring occasionally so the bottom doesn't burn.

3. Reduce the heat to low and add the rest of the dashi and the nira. Mix and gently cook for approximately 5 to 10 minutes, stirring occasionally, until the mixture has thickened. Turn off the heat and stir in the miso and soy sauce. All miso have different tastes, so add bit by bit and keep tasting until you have the flavor you want

4. Add salt to taste, ladle the soup into bowls, and serve hot.

NOTES

 To incorporate the miso, place into a small fine-mesh strainer and lower into the zousui. Use a spoon to mix and dissolve the miso. If you see any remains (rice koji) in the mesh, feel free to add into the zousui or discard.

 Zousui is typically a thin soup. However, miso thickens the mixture, so feel free to add more dashi to achieve the consistency you want.

Hearty
SHEPHERD'S PIE

Shepherd's pie is a classic British dish, more like a casserole than a pie. A ground lamb mix filled with herbs and vegetables is topped with smooth and cheesy mashed potatoes, then baked until the top is crisp and the inside is piping hot. This comfort food brings nostalgia to many, so you can sit and reminisce about the good times with your family! It's the perfect dish to enjoy after a hard day working for a witch in need of an extra pair of hands or scheming with your cat familiar friend. It will surely make you want bite after bite!

Serves: 6 | Prep time: 20 minutes | Cook time: 1 hour

INGREDIENTS

Mashed Potatoes

1¾ pounds russet potatoes

1 cup whole milk

4 ounces (¼ pound) unsalted butter

2 medium egg yolks

kosher salt and freshly ground white pepper

2 ounces parmesan cheese, grated

MASHED POTATOES

1. Peel the potatoes and cut into quarters.

2. Fill a medium saucepan halfway with water, season with a generous pinch of salt, and bring to a boil on the stovetop over medium-high heat. Add the potatoes and cook until tender enough to be easily pierced with a fork.

3. Drain the potatoes and let rest in the pan for a couple of minutes to let any remaining water drain off. Then transfer to a bowl and mash, using a potato ricer or masher.

4. Heat the milk and butter in a small saucepan over low heat until the butter has melted. Then slowly and gently stir into the potatoes using a rubber spatula. Season the potato mixture with salt, white pepper, and 1¼ ounces grated parmesan cheese. Thoroughly mix in the egg yolks, but don't overmix or the potatoes may become gummy. Set aside.

Lamb Filling
1 large onion
1 small carrot, peeled
½ celery stick
2 sprigs rosemary
3 sprigs thyme
1 pound ground lamb
kosher salt and freshly
ground white pepper
vegetable oil
4 cloves garlic
3 tablespoons tomato paste
1¼ cups dry red wine
2 tablespoons
Worcestershire sauce
1¼ cups beef stock
1 cup frozen green peas

LAMB FILLING

1. Dice the onion and carrot into small pieces. Finely slice the celery, and chop the rosemary and thyme. Place everything in separate small dishes and set aside.

2. Season the ground lamb with 1 tablespoon of kosher salt and ½ tablespoon black pepper and cook in a deep saucepan over high heat to achieve a golden-brown crust, breaking up the lamb as it cooks. If the heat is too low, the lamb will start to boil instead of fry, resulting in a dull grey color, and water will start coming out of the meat. Remember, color is flavor! Once the lamb is golden brown, transfer it to a bowl and set aside.

3. In the same pan, add a splash of vegetable oil and cook the onion pieces over medium heat until translucent. Scrape the bottom of the pan using a wooden spatula to remove any meat caught there. Add the celery and carrot pieces and mince in the garlic. Season with ½ teaspoon of kosher salt and cook for 5 minutes, stirring occasionally. Then add the cooked lamb and mix everything together.

4. Mix in the tomato paste and cook for 2 more minutes to remove its tartness, stirring every so often. Then pour in the wine and scrape the bottom of the pan. Let boil for a couple of minutes, until the alcohol smell has disappeared.

5. Add the chopped thyme, rosemary, and Worcestershire sauce. Pour in the beef stock and bring to a boil. Once boiling, reduce the heat to low and let simmer. Add the frozen peas and continue to simmer until the mixture has thickened enough to coat the back of a spoon.

6. Once the lamb mix has reached the desired consistency, slowly season it with salt, pepper, and sugar (if needed) to taste. Add small pinches of everything, taste, and then adjust accordingly. Remember, you can always add more, but you can't take away!

ASSEMBLY

1. Preheat the oven to 375°F. Place the lamb mix in a 9 x 9-inch casserole dish until it reaches halfway up the sides; press down with a spatula so there are no gaps.

2. Add the mashed potatoes on top, spreading them out evenly. Then sprinkle on parmesan cheese to cover completely. Using a fork, scrape along the top to make lots of rough edges; these will crisp up in the oven.

3. Place in the oven and cook for 30 minutes, or until the top is golden brown. Then remove and let sit for 5 minutes. Divide into portions to serve.

NOTES

- There are many components to this dish, so it's helpful to place the ingredients in separate bowls to keep everything organized!
- After frying the lamb, lots of brown bits will be stuck to the bottom of the pan. This is known as "fond" and contains lots of umami! Don't wash it away—add your onions straight into the pan to increase the depth of flavor when they are fried.
- While shepherd's pie doesn't traditionally include celery, it adds depth and a slight sweetness. Slicing the celery as fine as possible makes it dissolve into the mixture.
- If you don't want to use wine, you can add more beef stock instead.
- If you wish, you can use ground beef instead of ground lamb, which will make a variation of Shepherd's Pie known as Cottage Pie!

Tales of
TOMATO SOUP

After a long day of rescuing people from slave-traders, traveling across deserts, and restoring balance to the kingdom, there's no better way to warm up and revitalize yourself than with a classic tomato soup. Packed with nutrients and potatoes to keep you energized, this tomato soup is simple yet delicious!

Serves: 5 | Prep time: 10 minutes | Cook time: 30 minutes

INGREDIENTS

¾ pound unpeeled baby potatoes

2½ pounds ripe tomatoes

2 tablespoons extra-virgin olive oil

1 tablespoon unsalted butter

1 large onion, diced

1¼ cups vegetable stock

1 bunch basil, chopped, plus more for garnish

kosher salt, to taste

freshly ground white pepper, to taste

sugar, if needed

1. Wash and cut the potatoes in quarters or bite-size pieces, depending on the size of your potatoes. Next, boil in salted water over medium-high heat for 5 to 10 minutes until a fork easily pierces them. Drain and set aside.

2. For larger tomatoes, cut in quarters; for smaller ones, cut in halves. Place in a large bowl and add 2 generous pinches of salt, pepper, and 2 tablespoons olive oil. Toss with tongs or a rubber spatula until well coated. Place on a roasting tray and cook in the oven at 450°F for 10 minutes, or until the tomatoes are slightly charred.

3. In a medium saucepan over medium-low heat, heat the butter and diced onions for 10 minutes, stirring frequently. Season with salt and pepper to taste. Add the roasted tomatoes to the pan, including all the juices. Pour in the 1¼ cups vegetable stock, increase to a medium-high heat and bring to a boil.

4. Once boiling, lower the heat, stir in the chopped bunch of basil, and simmer for 5 minutes.

5. Transfer the sauce to a blender and mix until smooth. Then return the mixture to the saucepan and season with salt and pepper to taste. If the tomatoes taste sour, add ½ teaspoon of sugar at a time, while tasting, until the sourness has reduced.

6. Add the potatoes to the tomato soup mixture and heat in the soup for 2 minutes on low heat.

7. Serve in bowls and top with more basil, a crack of black pepper, and a small drizzle of olive oil.

NOTES

- Tomatoes have varying tastes, depending on the type, size, and season. Keep tasting as you are making the soup and adjust the seasoning accordingly. Tomatoes can take a lot of salt, so be generous!
- Add more stock if you prefer your soup a little thinner.
- Cooking the onions slowly will release their natural sweetness, so be patient and treat them with care.

Japanese Street-Style Fried Squid
(IKAYAKI)

Ever wanted to experience a Japanese festival? Well, now you can with this recipe! Fried squid, known as ikayaki in Japanese, is a classic street food found all over the country. Grilled over charcoal to add a hint of smokiness, this squid is irresistibly delicious. Finished with a dab of Kewpie mayonnaise and shichimi spice, ikayaki will have you living the Japanese festival dream without transforming you into a literal pig!

Serves: 4 | Prep time: 1 hour | Cook time: 6 minutes

INGREDIENTS

2 large squid, with tentacles

2 tablespoons Japanese cooking sake (see notes for substitute)

2 tablespoons mirin

2 tablespoons soy sauce

1 tablespoon grated ginger

1 teaspoon neutral-flavored cooking oil

Kewpie mayonnaise (optional)

Shichimi spice (optional)

1. Prepare the squid by using your hands to gently removing the heads and tentacles. Make sure to remove the spine, which looks like a long shard of plastic. Then rinse the insides under gently running cold water.

2. Remove the tentacles from the heads and cut them in half; discard the heads. Score the flesh in ½-inch integrals on the top of the squid, but don't cut all the way through.

3. Place the squid and the tentacles in a ziplock bag along with the sake, mirin, soy sauce, and ginger. Remove as much air as possible and seal the bag.

4. Mix everything together by rubbing the bag with your hands, then refrigerate for 1 hour to marinate.

5. Pour cooking oil into a medium to large frying pan.

6. Remove the squid from the plastic bag and hold it up with a pair of tongs to let the excess marinade drip off. Then fry over medium heat for 3 minutes. If it starts to curl up or move around, press it down with a spatula to keep it flat. Then flip over and fry for another 3 minutes.

7. Serve with Kewpie mayonnaise and shichimi spice.

NOTES

- If you are buying from a fishmonger, ask to have the squid cleaned so it's ready for cooking. Make sure to ask them not to cut the squid open but to keep it whole.
- If you can't find mirin, substitute with 2 tablespoons of sake mixed with 2½ teaspoons of sugar.
- To re-create the true taste of Japanese ikayaki, try grilling it over charcoal!

Japanese Street-Style Sweet Corn
(YAKI TOMOROKOSHI)

Who doesn't love corn on the cob during the warm summer, grilled over charcoal and doused with a sweet soy sauce mixture until charred and sticky? If that doesn't sound delicious enough, this version is also coated in butter, making a classic Japanese combination!

Serves: 4 | Prep time: 5 minutes | Cook time: 20 minutes

INGREDIENTS
4 ears sweet corn
3½ tablespoons soy sauce
4 tablespoons sugar
2½ tablespoons mirin
unsalted butter

1. Bring a large saucepan of water to a boil over high heat.

2. Remove any discolored outer layers of the corn husks. Then boil the corn with the husks on for 10 to 15 minutes, depending on the freshness and size of your corn. After 10 minutes, remove one ear and poke it with a sharp knife. If ready, the kernels should be bright yellow and show little resistance. If they still feel hard, cook for another couple of minutes. Then remove from the hot water and place on a tray to cool.

3. While the corn is cooling, combine the soy sauce, sugar, and mirin in a small bowl and whisk together.

4. Once the corn is cool enough to handle, remove and discard the husks. In a large frying pan, melt 2 tablespoons unsalted butter over medium heat. Using tongs, add the corn and turn so the cobs are covered in butter.

5. Add the soy sauce mixture to the pan and bring to a boil while rolling the corn around. Once boiling, reduce to a low heat. The sauce will start to thicken, coat the corn all around, and slightly char it.

6. Remove the corn from the pan and top the ears with more butter. Enjoy!

NOTES

- Boiling the corn in its husks helps retain its sweetness and color. If you prefer to remove the husks before boiling the corn, the cooking time will be shortened.

- Alternatively, you can microwave your corn. Soak the husks in cold water and then wrap individually in wet paper towels. Microwave at 600 watts for 5 minutes, then turn them over, still wrapped in the wet paper towels, and microwave for another 5 minutes. The cooking time may vary depending on the power of your microwave and the size and freshness of your corn. Leave to cool for a couple of minutes, remove the husks, and proceed as per the recipe.

- If you're able to grill over charcoal, that will add a deep, smoky flavor that makes the corn even more delicious!

- If any sauce is left in the saucepan, use a brush to coat the corn with more of that delicious sweet and salty combination.

Margherita
FOCACCIA

The Transcontinental Flight Café features a number of Eastern- and Western-inspired pizza dishes, including pizza! This recipe is a take on the park's Margherita pizza served on a fluffy focaccia crust.

Serves: 8 to 10 servings | Prep time: 10 minutes | Cook time: 50 minutes

INGREDIENTS

raw focaccia dough (page 13)

1 (28-ounce) can whole peeled San Marzano tomatoes, drained and juices reserved

3 large cloves garlic, grated

1 tablespoon kosher salt

½ tablespoon freshly ground black pepper

1 teaspoon sugar

8 ounces fresh mozzarella, plus more for topping

extra-virgin olive oil

chopped basil leaves

NOTE

🍄 Take your time making the tomato sauce—it's one of the most important parts of the pizza.

1. Preheat the oven to 425°F.

2. Place the whole canned tomatoes in a large bowl. Stir in the grated garlic, 1 tablespoon kosher salt, ½ tablespoon black pepper, and 1 teaspoon sugar. Taste and add additional seasonings as needed. Using your hands, or with the back of a large spoon, squeeze and crush the tomatoes. (Or, if you prefer to have your sauce smooth, put everything in a blender and mix on high until smooth.) If the sauce seems too thick, mix in some of reserved juices from the canned tomatoes.

3. Use a spatula to spread the tomato sauce on top of the focaccia dough. Tear the mozzarella into pieces and place on top of the sauce. Add 2 tablespoons of extra-virgin olive oil on top.

4. Bake the pizza for 35 to 40 minutes on the middle rack of the oven until it's a deep golden brown and bubbling. Remove from the oven and allow to cool for about 10 minutes, then slice into squares and top with basil.

Four-Cheese FOCACCIA

Calling all cheese lovers! This is the ultimate cheese indulgence—a marriage of favorite cheeses on a light and airy homemade focaccia. If you want a sweet kick, add a drizzle of honey for an irresistible sweet and savory meal!

Serves: 8 to 10 | Prep time: 10 minutes | Cook time: 50 minutes

INGREDIENTS

raw focaccia dough (page 13)

mozzarella, provolone, gorgonzola, and fontina cheeses (½ to 1 cup each)

extra-virgin olive oil

freshly ground black pepper, to taste

honey (optional)

1. Preheat the oven to 425°F.

2. Tear or cut the cheeses into bite-size pieces and dot them onto the focaccia.

3. Bake for 35 to 40 minutes on the middle rack of the oven until the crust is a deep golden brown and the cheese is bubbling.

4. Remove the pizza from the oven, let cool on a rack for about 10 minutes, and then slice into squares. Top each piece with a splash of extra-virgin olive oil and a crack of black pepper, and drizzle on honey if you wish.

NOTES

- Experiment with your favorite cheeses! You want each cheese to have a unique taste so that you can enjoy the combination of flavors.

- To add a sweet kick, drizzle honey on top of your pizza. It complements the cheeses wonderfully!

Nagoya-Style
MISO KATSU FOCACCIA

Ghibli Park is located in the city of Nagoya, famous for a dish known as miso katsu—a classic Japanese breaded pork cutlet doused in an umami-rich miso sauce. Enjoy this delectable treat on top of fluffy focaccia bread!

Serves: 2 | Prep time: 20 minutes | Cook time: 10 minutes

INGREDIENTS

¼ head cabbage

2 tablespoons mirin

2 tablespoons sake (Japanese rice wine)

¼ cup dashi (page 7)

1 tablespoon sugar

2 to 3 tablespoons red miso

¼ cup flour

1 medium egg, beaten

½ cup panko breadcrumbs

pinch of salt

2 (1-inch-thick) boneless pork loin chops

neutral-flavored cooking oil, for deep-frying

salt and pepper

2 (3 x 5-inch) pieces cut from baked focaccia loaf (page 13)

1. Using a mandoline, shred the cabbage into thin slices; if you do not have a mandoline, slice the cabbage as thinly as you can with a chef's knife. When only a small part remains, slice thinly with a knife. Place the shredded cabbage in a bowl of cold water with ice cubes. This will remove some of its odor and keep it crunchy.

2. Place the mirin and sake in a small saucepan over medium heat. Bring to a boil and let boil for 30 seconds, until the alcohol has evaporated and the smell is gone. Add the dashi, sugar, and red miso and mix until thoroughly combined. Turn the heat to low and simmer for 3 minutes until thickened, stirring occasionally to keep the bottom from burning. Remove from the stovetop and set aside.

3. Place the flour, beaten egg, and panko breadcrumbs in separate bowls or on deep trays. Season the flour with a pinch of salt and mix in.

4. For the pork loin chops, use a knife to make 3 to 5 slits between the fat cap and the meat. This will keep the pork from curling up when deep-fried.

5. Using the back of the knife or a tenderizer, pound the meat on both sides. Season both sides of the pork with salt and pepper, then roll in the seasoned flour. Remove excess flour by gently tapping the pork pieces against the side of the bowl or tray.

6. Place the pork in the beaten egg to coat it all around. Hold each pork chop up to let the excess egg drip off. Then place the pork in the panko breadcrumbs, using your hand to press the breadcrumbs into the pork and making sure the whole pork chop is covered.

7. Add oil to a medium saucepan so it is not quite half full and heat to 350°F on the stovetop. Deep-fry the pork chops in the oil for approximately 5 minutes or until golden brown, flipping them halfway through (but avoid touching them too often).

8. Place the cooked pork chops on a wire rack and let rest standing upright on their sides for 2 minutes.

9. To serve, cover the top of the focaccia with miso sauce. Add the pork, top with more sauce and the finely sliced cabbage, and serve.

NOTES

🍄 To avoid making a mess, use alternate hands when you cover the pork with the breadcrumbs!

🍄 You can check the readiness of your oil by holding a chopstick upright in the center of the pan. If bubbles start to appear around it, the oil is ready.

🍄 Cooking time will vary depending on the thickness of your pork. The meat will also continue cooking while resting, so take it out a little early.

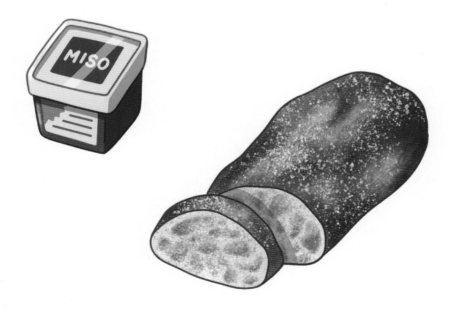

Seasonal
VEGETABLE FOCACCIA

A number of dishes found at the Ghibli Park are seasonal, meaning they are either available during certain times of the year or utilize certain seasonal ingredients. This recipe falls in the latter category; some classic seasonal vegetables to use are suggested, but you can use any that you like. Mix and match, but above all have fun!

Serves: 4 | Prep time: 10 minutes | Cook time: 50 minutes

INGREDIENTS

6 cherry tomatoes

2 to 3 slices each of seasonal vegetables (see below)

extra-virgin olive oil

kosher salt, to taste

freshly ground black pepper, to taste

2 stems rosemary, finely chopped

raw focaccia dough (page 13)

4 tablespoons parmesan cheese, grated

Spring Vegetables: asparagus, green peas, red onion

Summer Vegetables: zucchini, sweet corn, bell peppers

Autumn Vegetables: kabocha squash, butternut squash, carrots

1. Preheat the oven to 450°F.

2. Gather the cherry tomatoes and your favorite seasonal vegetables (see ingredients for suggestions). Create your own vegetable decoration and feel free to use however many of whichever vegetables you like. Peel as needed and cut the larger ones into bite-size pieces; leave the cherry tomatoes whole. Place in a large mixing bowl and add 2 tablespoons extra-virgin olive oil, a generous pinch of salt and pepper, and the chopped rosemary. Toss to coat everything with the oil.

3. Scatter the vegetables on the focaccia and top with another pinch of salt, more olive oil, and grated parmesan cheese.

4. Bake on the middle rack of a 450°F oven for 35 to 40 minutes, until the focaccia is a deep golden brown and the vegetables are cooked through.

5. Allow the focaccia to cool for about 10 minutes, then slice into squares and serve.

Classic Japanese Rice Ball (ONIGIRI)

Rice balls, known as onigiri, are a staple food in Japan. Whether you're looking for a quick snack or something to take to work for lunch, onigiri will always have your back. Along with the basic recipe, several popular fillings available at the park are included here.

Serves: 4 | Prep time: 5 minutes for the basic rice ball, plus extra time for fillings | Cook time: 10 minutes

INGREDIENTS

3 cups freshly cooked rice, slightly cooled (page 17)

water

table salt

roasted seaweed (nori)

SALMON FILLING

1 salmon fillet

kosher salt

SHRIMP TEMPURA FILLING

shrimp

potato starch, for dusting

½ cup cake flour

¼ cup ice water

OKAKA FILLING

¼ cup dried bonito flakes

1 tablespoon soy sauce

1 teaspoon sesame seeds

1. Divide the 3 cups of cooked white rice into quarters.

2. Fill a small bowl with water and mix in a pinch of salt. Wet your hands with the salt water, then scoop about ⅔ cup of the cooked rice into your left hand. If you want to add a filling, place them in the middle at this point. Filling recipes can be found on the next page.

3. Form a V-shape with your right hand and start to shape the onigiri, gently pressing the rice together. The right hand should always be in this V shape, on top of the rice.

4. Once a point forms on top, rotate the onigiri toward you and press again with your right hand to form another corner. Repeat until you have a triangular shape. Don't press too hard or you'll squash the rice together and ruin the onigiri texture. It should all just about come together and not fall apart when you hold it.

5. Wrap with seaweed, then repeat the process with the remaining rice.

SALMON FILLING

1. Season the salmon fillet with salt on both sides. Set on a baking pan and place in a 425°F oven for 10 minutes until tender.

2. Use a pair of spoons to break the salmon into flakes.

SHRIMP TEMPURA FILLING

1. Shell the shrimp, then make a slit down the back with a sharp knife. Use a wooden skewer and poke underneath the vein. Pull up and take the vein out.

2. Rinse with cold water, then pat dry with paper towels and dust with potato starch. Tap between your hands to remove excess potato starch.

3. In a small bowl, use a whisk to mix 1 tablespoon potato starch, the cake flour, and the ¼ cup ice water. Don't overwhisk—it's okay to have some lumps.

4. Use tongs to dip each shrimp in the mixture, then deep-fry in a medium saucepan at 350°F for about 2 minutes. Set aside on a wire rack.

OKAKA FILLING

1. In a small bowl, mix together the bonito flakes, soy sauce, and sesame seeds.

NOTES

🍄 Rice is the most important ingredient, so carefully follow the recipe on page 17.

Onigiri Set Meal
(ONIGIRI TEISHOKU)

You can find set menus known as teishoku at restaurants all over Japan, typically consisting of rice, soup, and some form of protein. This particular recipe inspired by a set menu found at the Rotunda Kazegaoka combines umami-packed pork miso soup with classic onigiri, perfect for a speedy refuel within a tight schedule.

Serves: 2 | Prep time: 20 minutes | Cook time: 20 to 30 minutes

INGREDIENTS

neutral-flavored cooking oil

5 to 7 ounces pork belly with skin removed, cut in thin slices (see notes)

½ fresh burdock root (gobo)

½ onion

3½ ounces daikon radish, peeled

½ medium carrot, peeled

1 green onion

4 cups dashi, or as needed (page 7)

5 tablespoons miso paste, plus more if needed

1 teaspoon grated fresh ginger

7 ounces tofu

1 green onion, thinly sliced

onigiri (page 61)

Japanese pickles or tsukemono (optional)

1. Wash the burdock root under water with a sponge to remove any dirt. Cut into the tip of the root to make small shavings, as if sharpening a pencil. Place the shavings in a small bowl of cold water and set aside.

2. Cut the onion in half and then into ¼-inch crosswise slices.

3. Peel the daikon radish and cut in quarters, then cut each quarter into roughly ¼-inch slices. Slice the carrot into similar-size pieces.

4. Slice the green onion diagonally into ½-inch pieces.

5. Add cooking oil to a deep saucepan over medium-high heat, just enough to cover the bottom. Add the pork belly slices and fry until cooked through. As they are thin slices, they will only take 45 seconds or so on each side.

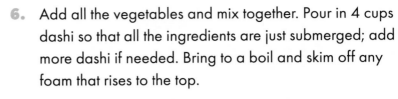

6. Add all the vegetables and mix together. Pour in 4 cups dashi so that all the ingredients are just submerged; add more dashi if needed. Bring to a boil and skim off any foam that rises to the top.

7. Cover with a lid and turn the heat to low. Simmer for 10 minutes, or until the vegetables are tender. Then place the miso paste in a strainer or ladle, lower it until it's just in contact with the soup, and use a whisk to mix it in. This will help fully dissolve the miso paste into the soup without leaving any lumps.

8. Add the grated ginger and taste. If it seems too strong, add more dashi. If it's too weak, add more miso.

9. Finally, cut the tofu into bite-size cubes and add it to the soup. Gently mix, ladle into two bowls, and top with sliced green onions. Serve along with the onigiri and some Japanese pickles.

NOTES

- You can find finely sliced pork belly in Asian supermarkets or you can ask your butcher to slice for you. If you want to slice yourself, place the pork belly block in the freezer for an hour to harden. Using a sharp knife, cut into 2-millimeter-thick slices.

- Prep all the vegetables before cooking and place on a tray or plate. Staying organized will help make the cooking process a lot easier and stress-free!

- Cutting the onions, carrots, and daikon radishes the same size is important to make sure they cook in the same amount of time.

- Burdock root, also known as gobo, adds an earthy flavor to the soup. It's traditional to add it, but you can leave it out If you can't find any.

- Avoid boiling the soup once the miso is mixed in, as that will ruin the flavor of the miso.

On-the-Go
ONIGIRI BENTO

This is the perfect bento box, whether you're packing your work lunch, preparing for a picnic, or hurrying between exciting anime-themed theme park attractions!

Serves: 4 | Prep time: 1 hour | Cook time: 20 minutes

INGREDIENTS

Tamagoyaki (Omelet)
3 large eggs
2 teaspoons sugar
1 teaspoon soy sauce
½ teaspoon kosher salt
neutral cooking oil

Japanese Fried Chicken
2 boneless chicken thighs
1 tablespoon soy sauce
1 tablespoon sake (Japanese rice wine)
½ teaspoon freshly grated ginger
1 clove garlic, grated
3 tablespoons flour
3 tablespoons potato starch
neutral cooking oil for deep-frying

Add-ons
8 small wieners
onigiri (page 61)
4 cherry tomatoes
Japanese pickles or tsukemono (optional)

TAMAGOYAKI

1. Use a whisk to mix together the eggs, sugar, soy sauce, and a pinch of salt in a small bowl.

2. Pour a small amount of neutral cooking oil into a separate small bowl. Fold a paper towel into a square and dip it in the oil. Place a rectangular tamagoyaki omelet pan (or use a small circular frying pan) on the stovetop over medium heat and wipe with the oiled paper to coat lightly.

3. Add ⅓ of the egg mixture and roll the pan to spread it out over the bottom of the pan. Using chopsticks, poke any air bubbles that form, then run the chopsticks along the edges of the pan to release the egg.

4. Fold the egg mixture over and push it to the top of the pan. Then, use the oiled paper towel to wipe more oil onto the pan surface.

5. Add another ⅓ of the egg mixture. Lift the cooked egg up and tilt the pan so the raw egg reaches underneath. Repeat until all 3 eggs have been cooked. You should be left with a rolled omelet!

JAPANESE FRIED CHICKEN

1. Cut the chicken thighs into bite-size pieces. Place in a large ziplock bag or medium bowl along with the soy sauce, sake, grated ginger, and garlic. Cover and let marinate for at least 1 hour in the refrigerator.

2. Mix the flour and potato starch together on a tray. Dip each piece of chicken into the mixture to coat, tapping it between your hands to remove any excess flour.

3. Pour neutral oil into a deep saucepan and heat to 325°F. Deep-fry the chicken in batches for about 2 minutes per batch. Use tongs to remove the pieces from the oil and place them on a wire rack.

4. Increase the heat to 350°F and deep-fry the pieces in batches again for 1 minute until they are golden brown and crisp, then remove from the pan and set aside on a wire rack.

ASSEMBLY

1. Make a criss-cross cut at the top of each wiener sausage. Over medium-heat, fry the sausages in a small skillet until cooked through, about 3 minutes. The ends should curl up to create an octopus-like shape, a classic for Japanese bentos.

2. Place a thick slice of tamagoyaki, 2 pieces of the fried chicken, a wiener sausage, your favorite onigiri, a cherry tomato, and some pickles into each bento. Enjoy during your lunch break or picnic!

Winter One-Pot Hot Pot
(ODEN)

Even a theme park as magical as the Ghibli Park experiences the bitter cold of winter. This classic dish, known as oden in Japan, is a comfort food filled with flavor and nutrients to keep you warm and cozy on any cold day, whether braving colorful attractions or snuggling up inside.

Serves: 4 | Prep time: 40 minutes | Cook time: 30 minutes

INGREDIENTS

4-inch daikon radish piece

4 large white potatoes

4 hard-boiled eggs, peeled

1 (6-ounce) block of konnyaku (yam jelly)

1 (12-ounce) pack of firm tofu

½ pound beef tendons or chicken thighs

fish cake selection (optional, see notes on page 72)

4 onigiri (page 61), to serve with the hot pot

PREPPING INGREDIENTS

1. Start by peeling the daikon and cutting it into 1-inch pieces; round the corners to help keep the desired shape. Score one side of the daikon pieces in a cross shape to help them absorb the broth.

2. Parboil the daikon in a small pan of water, uncovered, over medium-high heat for 15 to 20 minutes. Remove from the pan and set aside on a tray.

3. Peel the potatoes and cut in half (in quarters for larger potatoes). Place in a pan of water and parboil over medium-high heat until just slightly firm, about 10 minutes. The potatoes will be cooked again in the miso broth so should still be slightly hard. Remove from the water and set aside on the tray with the daikon.

4. Score the konnyaku in a crisscross pattern to help it absorb the miso broth, then cut into thirds and slice each piece in half diagonally to create 2 triangles.

MISO BROTH

4 cups dashi (page 7)

1 tablespoon sake
(Japanese rice wine)

1 tablespoon mirin

1 tablespoon soy sauce

1 teaspoon sugar

6 tablespoons miso paste
(see note on page 72)

Place in a medium saucepan of water over medium-high heat and boil for 30 seconds, then strain and set aside.

5. Cut the beef tendons or chicken thighs into bite-size pieces. Parboil in a medium sauce pan of water for 5 minutes over medium heat. Strain and set aside.

6. If including the fish cakes, parboil them in a pan of water for 30 seconds, then strain and set aside.

MISO BROTH

1. Add the sake, mirin, soy sauce, sugar, and dashi to a large saucepan and bring to a boil over medium-high heat.

2. Reduce to low heat and stir in the miso paste. Using a strainer or ladle, lower the miso until it is just in contact with the soup, then use a whisk to mix it in. This will help fully dissolve all the miso paste into the soup.

COOKING THE ODEN

1. Transfer all the prepared ingredients and the boiled eggs into a large pot. Ladle in the miso broth to just cover the ingredients. Slowly bring to a boil over medium heat, skimming off any scum that rises to the top.

2. Once boiling, turn the heat to the lowest level so the contents are just barely bubbling, then let simmer for 20 minutes uncovered, or until all the vegetables are tender.

3. Taste the broth and add more miso or dashi to taste. Serve in individual bowls alongside freshly made onigiri.

NOTES

🍄 Red miso paste is traditionally used in miso oden. Its bold, pungent, and umami-packed flavor makes the oden rich and luxurious. However, you can also use yellow miso, which is more mellow and balanced in flavor, with a hint of sweetness.

🍄 It's traditional to include various fish cakes in oden. You can find variety packs in Asian supermarkets. Alternatively, you can leave out the fish cakes entirely.

🍄 If you have the time, cover the surface of the cooled oden with a paper towel and then cover the pot with plastic wrap. Refrigerate overnight, allowing the miso broth to soak into each ingredient. To serve, bring the oden back to a simmer on the stovetop and cook until the ingredients are hot.

Perfect-Bite
BLT

A classic BLT (bacon, lettuce, and tomato sandwich) is so simple yet delivers on all levels. Salty and crispy bacon is paired with refreshing tomato and lettuce and finished off with mayonnaise flavored with a hint of garlic, all on a crisp but fluffy roll to create a sandwich that's just as scrumptous as the one at Ghibli Park's Transcontinental Flight Café.

Serves: 2 | Prep time: 5 minutes | Cook time: 20 minutes

INGREDIENTS

6 slices bacon

2 sandwich rolls (page 20)

lettuce leaves

1 large tomato

6 tablespoons mayonnaise

1 small clove garlic, grated (optional)

kosher sea salt, to taste

freshly ground black pepper, to taste

1. Cook the bacon in a 375°F preheated oven or in a frying pan on the stovetop. For the oven method, place the bacon strips on a baking tray lined with aluminum foil; set in the oven for 10 minutes, then flip and cook for another 10 minutes, or until your desired crispiness is achieved. For the stovetop method, cook slowly over medium to low heat until crispy. Place the cooked bacon on a tray lined with paper towels to drain off the excess fat.

2. Slice the rolls in half. Using the leftover bacon fat in the frying pan or oven tray, rub the cut sides of the rolls. You can lightly toast the bread in the frying pan or in the oven.

3. Place the lettuce leaves in a bowl of ice-cold water to crisp them. Slice the tomato into ¼-inch pieces.

4. In a small bowl, combine the mayonnaise and grated garlic. Spread a generous layer of the mayonnaise mixture on the insides of the rolls.

5. Place lettuce on the bottom rolls, then add the bacon and top with tomato slices. Season generously with kosher sea salt and black pepper. Cover with the roll tops and enjoy your sandwiches!

NOTES

🍄 You can use streaky bacon made from pork belly or back bacon made from the loin. Streaky bacon has more fat and crisps up; back bacon is meatier and won't crisp to the same degree. These come in separate packages so pick your preferred choice.

🍄 Garlic adds a punch to the mayonnaise, but feel free to leave it out if you prefer.

Hummus SANDWICH

This delicious and nutritious hummus sandwich hits all the right flavor notes, with hints of spices from smoked paprika and hearty ground cumin, complimenting a nutty and tangy chickpea blend. As quick and easy as it is to make, this is a perfect sandwich for a brief lunch break, especially during a long day of theme-park exploring!

Serves: 2 | Prep time: 10 minutes | Cook time: 5 minutes

INGREDIENTS

1 large zucchini

1 teaspoon ground cumin

½ teaspoon smoked paprika

1 large tomato

2 sandwich rolls
(page 20)

lettuce leaves

Hummus

2 medium cloves garlic, grated

zest and juice of 1 lemon, or as needed

ice-cold water

1 (12-ounce) can chickpeas, drained

6 tablespoons (3 ounces) tahini

1 teaspoon ground cumin

kosher sea salt, to taste

smoked paprika

extra-virgin olive oil

HUMMUS

1. In a food processor, blend together the grated garlic, lemon juice, and a couple tablespoons of ice-cold water.

2. Add the chickpeas, tahini, lemon zest, cumin, a pinch of salt, and a small drizzle of olive oil. Mix until well combined. If necessary, add a small amount of ice water until the right consistency is achieved.

3. When everything is blended, check the taste. Add salt and more lemon juice to your personal liking. Transfer to a bowl and set aside.

VEGETABLES

1. Place the lettuce leaves in ice-cold water.

2. Cut the zucchini into ¼-inch slices. Season with the ground cumin and smoked paprika and with salt and pepper to taste.

3. Place a frying pan or griddle pan on the stovetop over medium-high heat, add 1 teaspoon olive oil, and then,

add the zucchini slices. Cook for 30 to 60 seconds then turn the slices over and cook for another 30 to 60 seconds, or until tender.

4. Cut the tomato into ¼-inch slices. Generously season each slice with salt, pepper, and a drizzle of olive oil.

ASSEMBLY

1. Cut open the sandwich rolls and add drained lettuce leaves and tomato slices to the bottom halves.

2. Sprinkle on a generous amount of flaky sea salt and pepper, spread the hummus on top, and add a pinch of smoked paprika. Add the zucchini slices and cover with the tops of the rolls.

NOTES

🍄 If you want to make your hummus that extra bit smoother, place your canned chickpeas in a pan of water with 1 teaspoon baking soda over medium-high heat. Once boiling, reduce to low heat and simmer for 5 minutes. Strain and transfer the chickpeas to cold water. Use a strainer to remove as much of the chickpea skins as possible.

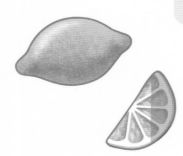

Tandoori
CHICKEN SANDWICH

Spicy, minty, and irresistibly delicious, this tandoori chicken sandwich makes for the perfect meal for a casual lunch date.

Serves: 2 | Prep time: 20 minutes | Marinating time: 12 hours | Cook time: 30 minutes

INGREDIENTS

2 ciabatta rolls (page 10)

½ large cucumber

¼ head of baby gem lettuce

TANDOORI PASTE

2 tablespoons ground coriander

2 tablespoons garam masala

4 teaspoons ground cumin

4 teaspoons ground turmeric

1 teaspoon Kashmiri chili powder (or regular chili powder)

10 cloves garlic

1 large ginger knob

2 tablespoons neutral-flavored cooking oil

¼ cup water, as needed

1. In a food processor or blender, combine the tandoori paste ingredients except for the water. Blend until a paste forms, then add up to ¼ cup water as needed to smooth the paste.

2. Lightly score the flesh of the chicken thighs to help with the marination. Then combine the chicken, 6 table-spoons tandoori paste, the yogurt, the lemon juice, and 1 tablespoon salt in a medium bowl. Using both hands, or a pair of tongs, thoroughly mix together so the marinade completely covers the chicken pieces. Cover and refrigerate overnight.

3. Set your oven to 450°F. Line a baking tray with aluminum foil and place a wire rack on top. Add the marinated chicken pieces on the highest rack, and grill in the oven for 20 minutes, or until cooked through. You want the chicken to have a slight char, so increase the heat if needed.

MARINADE

2 pounds boneless chicken thighs

6 tablespoons tandoori paste (above)

1 cup plain yogurt

zest and juice of 1 lemon

1 tablespoon kosher salt

SAUCE

¼ cup mayonnaise, or more as needed

small bunch of mint, chopped

small bunch of cilantro leaves, chopped

1 tablespoon plain yogurt

1 tablespoon extra-virgin olive oil

1 small clove garlic, grated

kosher salt and pepper, to taste

RED CABBAGE SLAW

¼ pound red cabbage

½ granny smith apple, peeled

zest and juice of 1 lemon

kosher salt

4. While the chicken cooks, start making the sauce. In a small bowl, combine the mayonnaise, mint, cilantro, yogurt, olive oil, grated garlic, and a generous pinch of salt and pepper; add extra mayonnaise if needed. Set aside.

5. For the slaw, use a knife to finely slice the cabbage, then transfer it to a bowl. Grate in the apple with a coarse cheese grater, and then add the lemon zest and juice, a pinch of salt, and 2 tablespoons of the mayonnaise sauce to help bind everything together.

6. Cut the ciabatta rolls in half and toast in a 350°F oven for 1 minute until lightly toasted. Spread the mayonnaise sauce on both halves of the rolls. Add the tandoori chicken on the bottom halves, then the red cabbage slaw, and cover with the top halves. Enjoy!

NOTES

- Store leftover tandoori paste in an airtight container in the fridge for a week. Marinate and cook more chicken to make more sandwiches, or add the paste to your favorite curry.

- Instead of using red cabbage, you can mix up the filling by using avocados, lettuce, and cucumber.

Vegetarian-Friendly
GUACAMOLE SANDWICHES

This is a meat-free sandwich option perfect for satisfying your avocado cravings and hunger!

Serves: 2 | Prep time: 5 minutes | Cook time: 2 minutes

INGREDIENTS

lettuce leaves

3 tablespoons finely sliced red onion

2 ripe avocados

1 teaspoon finely diced jalapeño pepper

2 tablespoons finely chopped cilantro leaves

1 small clove garlic, grated

juice and zest of ½ lime

extra-virgin olive oil

2 sandwich rolls (page 20)

salted butter

1 large tomato, sliced

kosher salt, to taste

pepper, to taste

1. Place the lettuce leaves in a bowl of ice-cold water to help crisp them. In a separate bowl, place the sliced onion in ice-cold water to help reduce its sharp taste.

2. Cut the avocados in half and remove the seeds. Scoop out the flesh into a bowl. Using a fork, mash the avocados until they are the consistency you prefer.

3. Stir in the jalapeño, cilantro, grated garlic, lime juice and zest, and a drizzle of olive oil.

4. Take the lettuce out of the water and pat dry with paper towels.

5. Cut the rolls in half, lightly toast in an oven at 350°F and butter the cut sides of each roll. Add a layer of lettuce and sliced tomato to the bottom halves and season generously with salt and pepper.

6. Add the guacamole mixture and red onion slices. Cover with the top halves of the rolls, and dig in!

NOTES

🍄 Ripe avocados are the key to good guacamole. When you press one with your fingers, it should be soft but still hard enough to not leave an indentation.

Prosciutto and Cheese
SANDWICH

You might enjoy this kind of sandwich after a long day of exploring Ghibli Park. And just like the similar sammie at Transcontinental Flight Café, this ultimate combination of prosciutto and cheese bursts with flavor with every bite.

Serves: 2 | Prep time: 5 minutes | Cook time: 5 minutes

INGREDIENTS

extra-virgin olive oil, for frying

10 roma tomatoes

kosher salt and freshly cracked black pepper

2 sandwich rolls (page 20)

unsalted butter, for spreading

prosciutto slices

4 slices Swiss cheese (see note below)

arugula leaves

1. Heat a medium frying pan over medium-high heat. Pour in just enough olive oil to cover the bottom of the pan. Add the tomatoes and cook until they blister and soften. Transfer to a tray or plate, season with salt and pepper, and set aside.

2. Cut the rolls in half and butter both sides. Layer on as much prosciutto as you like on the bottom half of each roll. Cover with 2 slices of Swiss cheese and place in the oven under the broiler so the cheese slightly melts. Remove and sprinkle on pepper.

3. Place the cooked tomatoes on the cheese. Add a few leaves of arugula, cover with the top half of the sandwich roll. Press down gently to flatten the tomatoes and release all the juices inside, and enjoy your sandwiches!

NOTES

🍄 Other cheeses—such as emmental, provolone, gouda, and cheddar—work well for these sandwiches, too.

Saucy
SPAGHETTI SANDWICH

This spaghetti, known as Napolitan in Japan, is so simple but delivers on every note. A mixture of vegetables and sausages with a ketchup sauce might sound bizarre, but it's a delightful combination that will keep you going for bite after bite!

Serves: 4 | Prep time: 15 minutes | Cook time: 20 minutes

INGREDIENTS
⅓ cup ketchup

1 tablespoon Worcestershire sauce

1 tablespoon tomato paste

½ onion

¼ green bell pepper

3 button mushrooms

4 sausages (see notes on page 88)

½ pound (200 grams) spaghetti

extra-virgin olive oil

2 cloves garlic, minced

3 tablespoons grated parmesan cheese

kosher salt, to taste

freshly ground black pepper, to taste

4 ciabatta rolls (page 10)

butter, as needed

1. In a small bowl, mix together the ketchup, Worcestershire sauce, and tomato paste. Set aside.

2. Cut the onion half into thin slices. Remove the seeds from the bell pepper and then cut horizontally into slices about the same size as the onion slices. Cut the stems of the mushrooms off and then cut into similar slices.

3. Cut the sausages into diagonal slices about the same width as the vegetable slices.

4. Bring a large saucepan of water to a boil on the stovetop over medium-high heat. Season generously with salt. Add the pasta and boil according to the package instructions.

5. In the meantime, start making the sauce. Add just enough olive oil to coat the bottom of a large frying pan and place over medium-high heat. Add the minced garlic and cook, stirring for 30 seconds, until fragrant. Then add the onion and fry for 2 to 3 more minutes, stirring occasionally, until it is more translucent in color and softer in texture.

6. Add the sausage slices and fry for another minute. Add the green bell pepper and mushroom slices and fry for about 1 minute.

7. Use a measuring cup to scoop out some of the pasta water. Add around 3 tablespoons to the ketchup and tomato paste and stir to loosen, then add the mixture to the vegetables.

8. By now the pasta should be nearly cooked. About a minute before it's done, use tongs to transfer it into the pan with the sauce. Turn the heat to high.

9. Add 2 tablespoons of extra-virgin olive oil, some black pepper, and the parmesan cheese. Mix vigorously so that everything is well incorporated. Taste and add more salt, pepper, or ketchup if needed, then set aside.

10. Cut the ciabatta rolls in half and toast in a 350°F oven for 1 minute until lightly toasted. Spread butter on the heated rolls and then spread on the pasta the bottom half and finish with the top roll.

NOTES

🧄 Traditionally, small wieners are used for Japanese Napolitan pasta, but feel free to substitute any kind of sausage, bacon, or ham that you wish.

🧄 If you have any leftover pasta, try making the Napolitan Quiche (page 111).

Spinach and Mushroom
SANDWICH

Spinach, mushrooms, and cheese—what's not to love? This delicious no-fuss sandwich hits all the right notes—sweet balsamic vinegar, gooey melted cheese, and a hearty helping of bacon will make your taste buds sing.

Serves: 2 | Prep time: 10 minutes | Cook time: 20 minutes

INGREDIENTS

1 cup balsamic vinegar

8 ounces fresh mushrooms (see notes)

2 bacon slices

extra-virgin olive oil

½ shallot, finely diced

1 large clove garlic, minced

1 teaspoon chopped fresh thyme leaves

2 tablespoons unsalted butter, plus more for buttering bread

kosher salt

black pepper

5 ounces baby spinach

2 (8 x 5-inch) baked focaccia slices (page 13)

4 slices provolone cheese

1. Add the balsamic vinegar to a small saucepan. Bring to boil over medium heat and let simmer until large bubbles form and the vinegar has reduced by about half. This will make the balsamic vinegar sticky and sweet.

2. Slice the mushrooms and bacon into ¼-inch pieces.

3. Add a splash of extra-virgin olive oil to a medium skillet. Add the bacon and fry for 1 minute on medium-high heat, stirring frequently. Add the sliced mushrooms and diced shallot and cook for another minute or so, stirring frequently.

4. Add the minced garlic, chopped thyme leaves, and 2 tablespoons butter. Season to taste with salt and black pepper. Fry for another 2 to 3 minutes, stirring, or until the mushrooms are golden brown.

5. Mix in the spinach and add another pinch of kosher salt. The spinach will cook quickly—it should take just 30 seconds to a minute. Remove the pan from the heat when it has cooked.

6. Slice the two focaccia pieces in half crosswise, and butter both sides. Add the spinach and mushroom mix on the bottom half. Layer on provolone cheese until the spinach mix is covered, then grill in the oven until the cheese has melted.

7. The balsamic vinegar should have cooled and become thicker by now. Drizzle it over the sandwiches and then cover with the top half of the focaccia.

NOTES

- There are no specific types of mushrooms you must use for this recipe—most kinds are suitable. Some recommendations are chestnut, portobello, cremini, and button mushrooms.

- The balsamic vinegar will give off a strong odor when simmering, so be sure to ventilate well! The reduction will thicken and harden as it cools. If it becomes too hard to drizzle, stir in a few drops of water until a syrup-like consistency is achieved. Any leftover vinegar will make a fantastic salad dressing, combined with some extra-virgin olive oil, lemon, salt, and pepper!

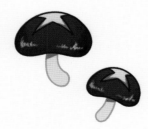

Mortadella
SAUSAGE FOCACCIA

This pizza-style focaccia like the one at Transcontinental Flight Café ticks all the right boxes—fluffy focaccia, rich tomato sauce, salty mortadella, and herby basil pesto creating a symphony of mouthwatering flavors and textures.

Serves: 6 to 8 people | Prep time: 20 minutes | Cook time: 50 minutes

INGREDIENTS
raw focaccia dough
(page 13)

16 slices mortadella
sausage

16 sprigs arugula

8 ounces fresh mozzarella,
plus extra for topping

Tomato Sauce
1 (28-ounce) can whole
peeled San Marzano
tomatoes, drained and
juices reserved

3 large cloves garlic

kosher salt

freshly ground black
pepper

sugar

TOMATO SAUCE

1. Transfer the whole canned tomatoes to a large bowl. Using a grater, grate the garlic into the bowl with the tomatoes and add salt, pepper, and sugar to taste. Using your hands, or a potato masher, squeeze and crush the tomatoes. If you prefer your sauce to be smooth, put everything into a blender and mix on high until smooth. If the mixture seems too thick, add some of the reserved juices from the canned tomatoes.

BASIL PESTO

1. Heat the oven to 350°F, place the pine nuts on a baking sheet, and roast until they are lightly golden brown—about 3 to 5 minutes.

2. Combine the basil and roasted pine nuts in a food processor or blender and mix until slightly broken down.

Basil Pesto

¼ cup pine nuts

2 cups fresh basil leaves

1 small clove garlic

¼ cup grated parmesan cheese

kosher salt

freshly ground black pepper

¼ cup extra-virgin olive oil

3. Add the garlic clove, parmesan cheese, a generous pinch of salt, and black pepper then mix again. While the food processor or blender is running, slowly pour in half of the olive oil. Use a rubber spatula to scrape down the sides and bottom, then repeat until everything is fully incorporated.

ASSEMBLY

1. Spread a thin layer of the tomato sauce on top of the focaccia dough. Using your hands, tear the mozzarella into small pieces and place on top. Add a splash of olive oil.

2. Bake in a 425°F oven for 30 to 40 minutes on the middle rack until a deep golden brown and bubbling. Remove and let cool on a cooling rack for about 10 minutes.

3. Slice into 5 inch squares (or your preferred size). Add small dots of the the basil pesto, slices of mortadella, any extra mozzarella and a few leaves of arugula for a peppery kick. Drizzle one teaspoon of extra-virgin olive oil on top and enjoy!

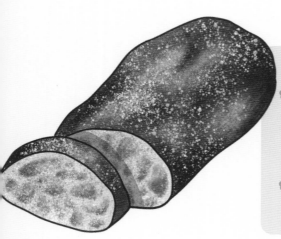

NOTES

- The key to a delicious mortadella sandwich is using the highest quality ingredients possible. This is a simple dish, so investing a little extra in the ingredients will go a long way!
- If you cannot find mortadella, you can use ham or salami instead.

Spicy Shrimp
SANDWICH

Spicy shrimp, creamy avocado, and punchy sriracha mayonnaise create the perfect show-stopper sandwich combination that unites the earth and the sea to satisfy your hunger and add a pep to your step!

Serves: 2 | Prep time: 20 minutes | Cook time: 10 minutes

INGREDIENTS
2 sandwich rolls (page 20)

¼ head lettuce

Guacamole
2 ripe avocados

3 tablespoons finely diced red onion

1 teaspoon finely diced jalapeño pepper

2 tablespoons finely chopped cilantro leaves

1 small clove garlic, grated

juice and zest of ½ lime

extra-virgin olive oil

Sriracha Mayonnaise
½ cup Kewpie mayonnaise (or regular mayonnaise)

2 tablespoons sriracha sauce

½ tablespoon honey

juice of ¼ lemon

1 small clove garlic, grated

kosher salt, to taste

GUACAMOLE
1. Cut the avocados in half and remove the seeds. Scoop out the flesh and place in a bowl. Using a fork, mash the avocados.

2. Stir in the red onion, jalapeño, cilantro, grated garlic, lime juice and zest, and a drizzle of extra-virgin olive oil.

SRIRACHA MAYONNAISE
1. In a small bowl, stir together the mayonnaise, sriracha, honey, lemon juice, grated garlic, and salt. Taste and add more of any of the ingredients, to your personal liking. Set aside.

SHRIMP
1. Shell the shrimp and make a slit down the back of each one using a sharp knife to expose the back vein. Insert a toothpick or skewer under the vein, then pull out and discard.

Chili Shrimp

1 pound raw shrimp

1 tablespoon smoked paprika

1 teaspoon cayenne pepper

1 teaspoon garlic powder

1 teaspoon ground cumin

½ teaspoon kosher salt

1 tablespoon unsalted butter

juice and zest of ¼ lime

3. Heat a frying pan over medium-high heat, then fry one side of the shrimp for about 2 minutes. Using tongs, flip the shrimp over and fry for another 1 or 2 minutes. Add the 1 tablespoon unsalted butter and the lime juice and zest and mix together. If you are using large shrimp, another couple of minutes of cooking time may be necessary.

4. Remove the shrimp from the pan, place on a tray or plate, and set aside.

ASSEMBLY

1. Cut the sandwich rolls in half and lightly toast both sides in a 350°F oven for 1 minute.

2. Spread the sriracha mayonnaise on the bottom half of each roll. Then add lettuce leaves and a generous layer of guacamole. Top with the spicy shrimp, drizzle on more sriracha mayonnaise to your liking, and add some more lime zest for a fragrant kick.

3. Cover with the top halves of the rolls.

NOTES

🍄 When cooking the shrimp, add them to the frying pan in a clockwise direction to help keep track of which ones get cooked first. Only flip the shrimp once, starting with the first one you place in the pan.

🍄 Use more or less chili powder and cayenne pepper than called for according to your own spice tolerance!

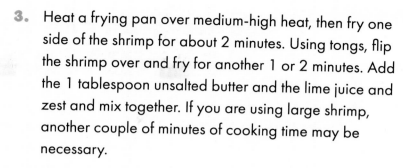

Sweet Bean and Butter
SANDWICH

The combination of sweet red beans (anko) and butter is a classic in Japanese desserts. You can find "anbutter" (short for anko and butter) sandwiches in many Japanese bakeries and even the park's Transcontinental Flight Café, but now you can make them in the comfort of your own home!

Serves: 2 | Prep time: 2 minutes | Cook time: 5 minutes

INGREDIENTS

2 ciabatta rolls (page 10)

6 tablespoons sweetened red bean paste (page 23)

6 to 8 thin slices of unsalted butter

1. Cut your ciabatta rolls in half and lightly toast both sides in a 350°F oven for 1 minute.

2. Spread a generous layer of sweetened red bean paste on the bottom half of the ciabatta roll. Add 3 to 4 thin slices of unsalted butter and add the top half of the ciabatta. Enjoy with a hot cup of coffee!

NOTES

🟣 It's traditional to use a thin slice of butter inside the sandwich. However, if that seems too rich, you can spread a generous amount of butter onto both sides of the ciabatta rolls to melt.

🟣 Try adding a few flakes of sea salt for a delicious sweet and salty balance!

Classic British
PORK PIES

Inspired by the witchy stall found in the Valley of Witches, these classic British pork pies explode with irresistible flavors with every mouthful. Tender pork encased in a crisp, golden pastry shell—how can it get any better than these ultimate showstoppers?

Makes: 4 to 6 (3-inch) pork pies | Prep time: 50 minutes |
Cook time: 50 minutes | Cooling time: 5 hours +

INGREDIENTS

Crust
6 ounces lard or unsalted butter

1 cup water

4½ cups all-purpose flour

2 teaspoons kosher salt

neutral-flavored cooking oil

2 egg yolks, for brushing crust

Pork Filling
1 pound boneless pork shoulder

6 ounces pork belly

3 sprigs thyme, leaves removed and chopped

4 sage leaves, chopped

½ teaspoon ground nutmeg

2 teaspoons kosher salt

1 teaspoon freshly ground black pepper

CRUST

1. Add the butter or lard and water to a small saucepan over medium heat until the butter is melted. Remove from the stovetop.

2. Combine the flour and salt in a large bowl, then pour in the melted butter mixture. Using a rubber spatula, mix until roughly combined and cooled down. Use your hands to knead the dough in the bowl until the flour and butter are completely mixed.

3. Lightly dust your work surface with flour, then knead the dough for 3 to 5 minutes until smooth; do not overwork. Cover with plastic wrap and refrigerate for 1 hour.

4. Remove the dough from the refrigerator and divide it into two pieces, ⅔ and ⅓ of the dough. Place the smaller portion back in the fridge.

Jelly

3 gelatin leaves

1 cup pork stock (or chicken stock)

kosher salt, to taste

freshly ground black pepper, to taste

SPECIAL EQUIPMENT

6 glass jars, 3 to 4 inches in diameter

twine

pastry brush

5. Roll the larger portion of the dough into about a ⅓-inch thickness, or slightly thinner. Cut out a dough circle about 6 inches wide (It doesn't have to be a perfect circle.)

6. Lightly brush neutral-flavored oil on the outside of a glass jar 3 to 4 inches in diameter. Set the jar in the middle of the dough circle and bring the dough up along the sides, checking to be sure the crust isn't too thin and that there are no holes; this will form the base and walls of your pie. If the dough tears, fill in the gaps with more pastry. The walls of the dough should be around 4 inches tall.

7. Cut a piece of parchment paper to fit around the jar and wrap it around the dough, securing it with twine and then gently removing the jar. Repeat for the rest of the dough portion. Transfer the shaped dough pieces to a parchment-lined baking sheet and chill in the refrigerator for 1 hour.

ASSEMBLING AND BAKING

1. While the dough chills, use a knife to finely dice the pork shoulder and belly. Place in a medium bowl and season with the thyme, sage, nutmeg, salt, and pepper.

2. Remove the shaped crust from the refrigerator and scoop in the pork filling, leaving roughly a ¼ gap at the top of each dough shell.

3. Take the remaining piece of dough out of the refrigerator and roll it to a ¼-inch thickness, then use your jar as a guide to cut out circles slightly larger than the pie for the pie lids. Use a pastry brush or your finger to brush water on the edges, then place the pastry circles on top of the filled pies and pinch together the edges. Use a

knife to poke a hole in the center of each pie to let the steam out while cooking.

4. Brush each the top and sides of each pie with egg yolk and add a sprinkle of kosher salt on top. Bake at 300°F for approximately 50 minutes, depending on the size of your pies. Use a cooking thermometer to check; the inside should be 175°F when fully cooked.

5. Remove the pies from the oven and set aside to cool for at least 45 minutes before adding the jelly.

JELLY

1. Soak the gelatin leaves in ice-cold water according to the package directions.

2. If you are using stock cubes, prepare the stock according to the package directions. If you are using stock cans, place over medium low heat in a small saucepan and add the gelatin to the stock and stir together.

3. Season to taste with a generous pinch of salt and black pepper. At this stage, the mixture should still be liquid.

4. Carefully pour the liquid jelly mix into the hole on top of each pie until it just starts to overflow. Refrigerate for at least 3 hours to let the jelly harden.

5. Take the pies out of the refrigerator, slice and serve with some Dijon mustard.

NOTES

🍄 You can also use an individual 4-inch springform cake pans to make each pie. Lightly brush the inside of the pan with a neutral oil, add the crust, and gently mold it to the pan. Add the pork filling and the pastry top. Cut a hole in the middle of the top. Then, bake for 300°F for approximately 50 minutes, let rest, and add the jelly according to the recipe. To make sure they can easily come out of the pans, run a knife around the edge, between the walls of the pie and pan. Set in the fridge for a minimum 3 hours. Before serving, unclip the springform to carefully release the pie.

🍄 Alternatively, you can make a single large pie using a 6 x 9-inch cake pan. This will increase cooking time to approximately 1 hour and 30 minutes.

🍄 These pies are traditionally served chilled, allowing the jelly inside to set. Serve your pies along with some Dijon mustard.

Beer Battered
FISH AND CHIPS

Deliciously crisp and flaky beer-battered fish, triple-cooked chips (more familiar to Americans as fries), and minty, mushy peas—enjoy this classic British dish that's similar to a crowd-pleaser on the spellbinding menu featured at the Flying OVEN.

Serves: 4 | Prep time: 1 hour |
Cook time: 30 minutes | Cooling time: 2 hours (see notes)

INGREDIENTS
Chips
6 large russet potatoes
4 lemon wedges for serving
kosher salt
2 to 4 cups of neutral oil for deep frying (fill until the pot is ⅓ full)

CHIPS

1. Cut the potatoes into thick, finger-size pieces. You can either keep the skin on or peel it off.

2. Add the potatoes to a large pot of cold water and set aside for 30 minutes to help remove some of the starch in potato.

3. Drain the starchy water with a large strainer. Fill the large pot with cold water, add the potatoes, and season generously with salt. Bring to a boil over high heat. Once it comes to a rigorous boil, slightly lower the heat so it is a gentle boil until the potatoes are just about falling apart, 10 to 15 minutes, stirring every 2 minutes. The boiling time will depend on the size of your potatoes so keep an eye on them.

4. Transfer the cooked potatoes to a wire rack or a tray lined with parchment paper to cool. Then chill in the freezer for 1 hour uncovered.

Tartar Sauce

1 cup mayonnaise

1 clove garlic, grated

1 large dill pickle, finely diced

1 tablespoon Dijon mustard

1 tablespoon capers

6 sprigs of fresh dill

kosher salt, to taste

Minty Mushy Peas

4 ounces frozen peas

½ shallot, finely diced

1 clove garlic, crushed

2 tablespoons unsalted butter, divided

¼ cup heavy cream

juice and zest of ¼ lemon

2 tablespoons chopped fresh mint

kosher salt

freshly ground black pepper

5. Fill a large pot ⅓ full with neutral cooking oil and heat to 285°F. Deep-fry the potatoes in batches for 10 minutes, or until they are slightly turning golden yellow. Avoid touching the potatoes as much as possible while deep-frying them, or they will start to break apart.

6. Using a large slotted spoon, transfer the potatoes from the hot oil to a wire rack or a tray lined with parchment paper. Let cool, then chill in the freezer for 1 hour.

TARTAR SAUCE

1. In a small bowl, combine the mayonnaise, grated garlic, diced dill pickle, mustard, and capers.

2. Finely chop the dill and add it to the sauce along with salt to taste. Cover and refrigerate until ready to serve.

MINTY MUSHY PEAS

1. Boil the frozen peas according to the package directions and then strain, discarding the water.

2. Finely dice the shallot and garlic.

3. Add 1 tablespoon of butter to a medium saucepan over medium heat, and then add the shallots. Once they start turning translucent, add the garlic and fry until it's fragrant.

4. Add the peas and use a potato masher to mash some of them; you want some mashed and some whole, for an interesting texture.

5. Stir in the cream, 1 tablespoon butter, mint, lemon juice and zest, salt, and pepper to taste. If the mushy peas seem too hard, add more cream or water. Set aside until serving.

Fish

4 (5-ounce) cod fillets, skin on

flour, for dredging

neutral oil for deep-frying

½ cup all-purpose flour

½ cup rice flour

½ teaspoon baking powder

1 teaspoon garlic powder

1 teaspoon paprika

1 teaspoon kosher salt

1 cup cold beer

FISH

1. Season the fish with salt on both sides. Place on a plate or tray, cover, and refrigerate for 10 minutes, uncovered.

2. For the beer batter, in a medium bowl, mix together the all-purpose and rice flours, baking powder, garlic powder, paprika, and kosher salt. Slowly stir in the beer. Don't overmix—it's fine to have some lumps. The consistency should be similar to custard. If it seems too thick, you can add more beer; If it's too thin, add more flour.

3. Remove the fish from the refrigerator and pat dry with paper towels. Sprinkle flour in a bowl or on a tray and generously season with salt. Place the cod pieces in the flour to coat all around.

ASSEMBLY

1. Lift and gently tap each fillet to remove excess flour, then place in the beer batter. Making sure the fish is completely covered, use tongs to pick each piece up by one end and hold it above the batter to let excess batter drip off. Then submerge about 1 inch of the cod in the oil for a few seconds. This will prevent the cod from sticking to the pan.

2. Using a fork or your fingers, drizzle some more of the batter on top of the fish as it is deep-frying. Deep-fry for 5 to 8 minutes, depending on the size and thickness of the fish; flip each piece halfway through. Using a pair of tongs, remove and place on a wire rack. Immediately sprinkle flaky sea salt on top.

3. Increase the oil heat to 375°F and deep-fry the chips for a couple of minutes until golden brown and crisp. Serve alongside the cod, mushy peas, tartar sauce, and lemon wedges.

NOTES

- Deep-fry the fish and chips in batches. As soon as you put something in the oil, it lowers the temperature. If you overcrowd the pot, it will never get back up to the correct temperature and won't deep-fry properly.

- The beer for the batter should be freshly opened and as cold as possible. This helps create lots of air in the batter and crisps the chips when deep-frying them.

- You can substitute sparkling water for the beer.

- The 2 hours of chilling time for the chips between stages is crucial for making them extra crisp on the outside and extra fluffy on the inside. If you don't have the time, however, you can skip the chilling steps.

Napolitan QUICHE

Once you've mastered the unique flavors of the Saucy Spaghetti Sandwich (page 87), put your Napolitan-making skills to the test with this hearty combination of Japanese comfort food and classic French dining inspired by the dish that is served by the witch-folk over at the park's Flying OVEN for lunch.

Makes: 1 (9-inch) quiche | Prep time: 20 minutes | Cook time: 40 minutes | Cooling time: 1 hour

INGREDIENTS

Crust
1½ cups all-purpose flour

1 teaspoon kosher salt

½ cup (1 stick) cold unsalted butter, cut in small cubes

2 to 4 tablespoons ice water

Filling
2 eggs, at room temperature

¾ cup heavy cream

1 teaspoon kosher salt

½ teaspoon freshly ground black pepper

½ cup grated cheddar cheese, divided

6 tablespoons grated parmesan cheese, divided

Napolitan pasta, chilled (page 87)

1 slice bacon

CRUST

1. Add the flour and salt to the food processor and pulse until combined.

2. Add half the cubed butter and pulse until mixed in. Then add the remaining butter and pulse again. The mixture will be crumbly, so add 2 to 4 tablespoons of ice-cold water until the crust starts to come together. You can check by gently squeezing the dough together; it shouldn't feel too wet or too dry. But touch the dough as little as possible to keep the butter from melting.

3. Immediately press the dough into a disc shape, cover with plastic wrap, and refrigerate for 1 hour.

4. Dust your work surface with flour and use a rolling pin to roll the crust to a ⅛-inch thickness. Make sure it is about 2 inches wider, all the way round, than your pie pan.

5. Place the crust in a 9-inch pie pan and use a ball of excess raw dough to press it into the pan; let the excess

fold over the sides. Scrunch a piece of parchment paper and place it on top of the crust, then refrigerate for 30 minutes. Preheat the oven to 350°F.

6. Place your baking beans or pie weights on top of the parchment paper and bake the crust for 15 to 20 minutes. It should start to develop a very light golden-brown color. Remove the baking beans and paper and return the crust to the oven for another 3 to 5 minutes, until the base is set and the color has deepened.

QUICHE FILLING

1. In a medium bowl, whisk together the eggs, cream, salt, and pepper. The mixture should be as smooth as possible, so don't over-whisk. Over-whisking will incorporate air into the filling, causing it to rise in the oven.

2. Mix in ¼ cup of grated cheddar cheese and 2 tablespoons of grated parmesan cheese.

BAKING

1. Add 2 tablespoons of the parmesan and ⅛ cup of cheddar cheese to the base of the quiche crust, then top with the Napolitan pasta so it fills up to half of the quiche. Add the quiche filling, leaving about a ⅛-inch gap at the top. Add a slice of bacon on top.

2. Bake in a 350°F oven for 20 minutes. Take the quiche out and top with the rest of the parmesan and cheddar cheeses.

3. Place back in the oven for another 20 minutes. Remove when the middle is just set; the sides should be firm, but the center should still have a little jiggle.

4. Allow to cool to room temperature. Slice into portions to serve.

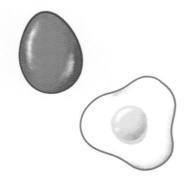

NOTES

- Touch the crust as little as possible while preparing the quiche. The heat from your hands will melt the butter, resulting in a hard and tough crust.

- Don't overwork the pastry. Pulse it in the food processor until everything just about comes together. Overworking will cause the crust to tighten and harden when baked.

- Do not overfill with pasta! It should be light and not too dense.

Spooky Roasted
BUTTERNUT SQUASH SOUP

Who doesn't love a good soup? Roasted butternut squash kissed with a blend of spices and blended with stock and coconut milk, this is the ultimate comfort dish perfect for outdoor adventures during the crisp autumn months.

Serves: 4 to 6 | Prep time: 20 minutes | Cook time: 50 minutes

INGREDIENTS

1 whole butternut squash

2 tablespoons olive oil

1 teaspoon nutmeg

1 teaspoon ginger

1 teaspoon ground cinnamon

1 teaspoon curry powder

1 whole garlic head

1 onion

3 tablespoons unsalted butter

4 cups chicken or vegetable stock, or as needed

½ cup coconut milk, plus more for topping the soup

homemade focaccia (page 13)

kosher salt, to taste

freshly ground black pepper, to taste

1. Preheat the oven to 425°F. Use a knife to cut the top off the butternut squash, then cut the squash horizontally into 2 pieces so you have a larger bottom part and a thinner top part. Stand each part up on its cut edge and carefully cut to remove the skin and divide both parts vertically in half. Use a spoon to scoop out and discard the seeds.

2. Roughly cut the squash into 1 to 2-inch cubes. Place in a large bowl and mix with the olive oil, nutmeg, ginger, cinnamon, and curry powder. Generously season with salt and pepper. Cut the garlic head in half, then place everything on a baking tray.

3. Roast the butternut squash for 25 minutes, or until tender and caramelized on top. It's important to get a nice caramelization, as that will increase the depth of flavor. If you find that the squash is not caramelizing, increase the oven heat.

Vegetable Add-ons

kabocha squash

3 russet potatoes

eggplant

red bell pepper

broccoli

cauliflower

maitake or button mushroom

zucchini

onion

neutral oil for deep frying

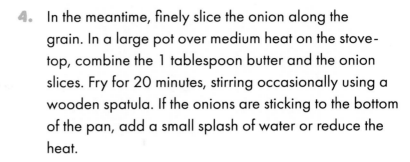

4. In the meantime, finely slice the onion along the grain. In a large pot over medium heat on the stovetop, combine the 1 tablespoon butter and the onion slices. Fry for 20 minutes, stirring occasionally using a wooden spatula. If the onions are sticking to the bottom of the pan, add a small splash of water or reduce the heat.

5. Add the cooked squash to the onions. Squeeze the garlic cloves from their skins (discard the skins) and add to the mix. Fry for about 2 minutes, stirring.

6. Add enough chicken or vegetable stock to just cover the squash. Bring to a boil and simmer, uncovered, for 15 minutes.

7. Add the soup to a blender in batches and blend until smooth. To make the soup even smoother, you can pass it through a chinois (conical sieve) or fine-mesh strainer.

8. Add ½ cup of coconut milk and mix. Add more coconut milk or chicken stock as necessary to achieve your desired consistency, along with 2 tablespoons of butter. Taste and season with salt and pepper as needed.

VEGETABLES

1. Peel the vegetables as needed or preferred. Cut the kabocha squash into ¼-inch slices, and cut the rest of the vegetables into bite-size pieces.

2. Boil the potatoes in a medium saucepan for 10 minutes or until they can easily be pierced with a knife with no resistance. Similarly, separately boil cauliflower for 30 seconds. Drain and place on a tray with kitchen paper to absorb any excess water.

3. Drain and then deep-fry each vegetable in a pot of 350°F oil on the stovetop. Each vegetable should take around 1 minute to cook so you can cook in batches, mixing the vegetables. Fry until golden brown and tender, then using a metal slotted spoon, remove and place on a wire rack set over a sheet pan to drain the excess oil.

4. To serve, fill individual bowls with the butternut squash soup and top with a piece of each vegetable and a drizzle of coconut milk. Add freshly ground black pepper and serve along with homemade bread.

NOTES

- If you can't find butternut squash, you can replace it with kabocha squash or even carrots. If you don't like coconut milk, simply use more vegetable stock instead.

- Roasting the garlic makes it turn deliciously sweet and reduces its pungent garlic flavor. Frying the onion is important, as a lot of natural sweetness is released as the onion slowly cooks. Your patience will be rewarded!

- Deep-frying vegetables this way is known as *suage* in Japanese—a common method used for curry soup.

- To make a really spooky soup, try adding some bamboo charcoal powder after blending!

Chapter 3

DESSERTS AND SWEET TREATS

Red Bean Pancake
(IMAGAWAYAKI)

Imagawayaki, or Obanyaki, is a classic street food sweet in Japan. It's been a staple in Japanese cuisine since the late eighteenth century, and with good reason. In a special cast iron pan, a pancake-style batter is fried to form a cylinder until golden brown and crisp on the outside and fluffy on the inside. If it couldn't get any better, then the Imagawayaki is traditionally stuffed with red bean paste or vanilla custard!

Traditionally, imagawayaki is made using a giant cast-iron pan with circular molds inside with a lid. Throughout Japan, you can find specialized shops and stalls where you can enjoy watching the Imagawayaki being expertly made. They are so popular that you can find them at festivals, department stores, convenience stores, supermarkets, and even frozen!

You can buy a special Imagawayaki pan online, some being cast iron and others ceramic and induction-friendly. The one used in this recipe is a ceramic pan with four circular molds, which will make two Imagawayaki at a time. If you can't find one, you can use sheet of foil folded until 2 inches thick, and formed and taped into a round shape.

Makes: 6 pieces (6 people) | Prep time: 1 hour 10 minutes | Cook time: 5 minutes

INGREDIENTS

2 medium eggs

1½ ounces sugar

½ teaspoon salt

2 teaspoons honey

1¼ cups whole milk

1 teaspoon baking powder

2 cups cake flour

10 ounces sweetened red bean paste (page 23)

1. In a large mixing bowl, use a whisk to combine the eggs, sugar, salt, and honey. Add the milk and mix in.

2. Add the baking powder and cake flour into the egg mix in stages to help incorporate better and reduce lumps. Don't whisk too much or gluten will develop and the dough will become tough. Use a whisk to gently mix everything together, then scrape the sides and bottom

Imagawaki pan
small metal spatula
sifter

of the bowl with a rubber spatula. Cover the bowl with plastic wrap and refrigerate for 1 hour.

3. In the meantime, weigh the red bean paste into 50-gram portions, about ⅓ cup each. Form each portion into a small disc, about half the diameter of the circular mold. Place on a tray, cover with plastic wrap and set aside in the fridge.

4. After the batter has chilled for an hour, gently mix it with a rubber spatula and then pour it into a measuring cup with a spout. This will make it easier to pour into the molds.

5. Heat the Imagawayaki pan on the stovetop over medium heat. Rub oil around all sides of the circular molds in the pan, using a paper towel.

6. Pour in batter to reach halfway up two of the circular molds and fry for 1 minute.

7. Pour batter halfway up the two remaining molds and fry for another 2 minutes, then place a portion of red bean paste in the center of these pancakes.

8. Gently run the end of a small metal spatula around the mold edges to help release the sides. Then flip the first two pancakes onto the ones containing the red bean paste. If any batter spills over, use the metal spatula to push it into the side of the pancake.

9. Gently press down on the top of each Imagaway-aki with the metal spatula to combine the two halves. Cook for 1 more minute. If you feel that the top has not cooked enough, flip the pancake over and cook for another minute or so.

10. Enjoy piping hot with a cup of coffee or tea, as an indulgent afternoon snack!

NOTES

- For Step 7, while a metal spatula will make it much easier to flip the Imagawayaki, you can also use an ordinary dinner knife.

- You can use chilled vanilla custard instead of the red bean paste. In that case the Imagawayaki will require a few more minutes of cooking.

- Eat the Imagawayaki as soon as possible to enjoy the crisp exterior and fluffy inside. You can also refrigerate them for up to 3 days, then warm them in a 350°F oven until the exterior is crispy.

Harajuku CREPES

Crepes are synonymous with Tokyo's fashion district, Harajuku. Walking along and admiring all the latest fashions, there's no better food to enjoy than this sweet crepe. Filled with cream, custard, and any kind of fruit you can imagine, it will satisfy any sweet craving. The crème pâtissière takes some patience and effort, but it makes the crepe that much more indulgent!

Serves: 4 | Prep time: 1 hour | Cook time: 5 minutes

INGREDIENTS
Pastry Cream (page 126)

Whipped Cream
1 cup whipping cream
1½ tablespoons confectioner's sugar

Crepe
2 medium eggs
2½ tablespoons granulated sugar
⅜ cup flour
⅓ cup plus 1 tablespoon whole milk
1 teaspoon vegetable oil
pinch of kosher salt
butter for cooking
24 strawberries or other fruit, cut in bite-size pieces

SPECIAL EQUIPMENT
electric whisk (optional)
piping bag and tip

1. Make the pastry cream (see page 126).

WHIPPED CREAM
1. While the pastry cream cools, combine the cream and confectioner's sugar in a mixing bowl and whisk with a hand mixer on medium-high speed until medium peaks form. Place in a piping bag and set in the refrigerator.

CREPE
1. Crack the eggs into a large bowl and add the 2½ tablespoons granulated sugar. Whisk to combine, then add the flour and mix until fully incorporated. Whisk in the milk, vegetable oil, and a pinch of salt.

2. In a large frying pan over medium-low heat, pour in ½ teaspoon of unsalted butter. Swirl the fry pan around so the bottom of the pan is covered in the butter. Add a ladle of the crepe mix and quickly tilt the pan all around so the batter covers the pan bottom. Cook for 1 minute, or until the crepe bottom is light brown. Then use a spatula or a table knife to release the edge of the crepe and flip it over. Cook for another 30 seconds.

3. Transfer the crepe to a plate and then repeat the process for the rest of the crepe mix. You can stack the crepes on top of each other as they are done.

4. To assemble, imagine that the crepe is a clock and spread a thick line of the pastry cream from 12 o'clock at the edge of the crepe to the center. Be generous! Next pipe whipping cream over the pastry cream. Then pipe a line of cream from 12 to 10 o'clock along the perimeter of the crepe.

5. Add 4 to 6 pieces of fruit to each crepe along the whipped cream. Then fold the right half of the crepe over. You should be left with a semi circle with the fillings at the top half of the crepe. Roll this part around the rest of the crepe to create a cone shape.

6. Pipe more whipped cream on top of each crepe and add more fruit. Serve with your favorite chocolate sauce!

PASTRY CREAM (CRÈME PÂTISSIÈRE)

INGREDIENTS

½ vanilla pod or 1 teaspoon vanilla extract

1 cup whole milk

3 medium egg yolks

4 tablespoons of superfine sugar

1½ tablespoons all-purpose flour

1½ tablespoons cornstarch

1. Slice the vanilla pod in half and scrape out the seeds, using the back of a knife or spoon. (You can add the vanilla pod for extra flavor, but remove it before adding the vanilla seeds to the egg mix.) Place the seeds (or vanilla extract) and the 1 cup milk in a small saucepan over medium-low heat until the mixture gently simmers. Stir with a rubber spatula so the bottom does not burn. Then set aside to allow the vanilla to infuse into the milk.

2. Place the egg yolks in a mixing bowl, add the fine sugar, and whisk with a hand mixer on medium-high speed until thick and pale yellow. Mix in the flour and cornstarch.

3. Slowly pour the infused milk into the egg mixture while continuously mixing with a hand whisk. Once combined, pass the mixture through a chinois or fine-mesh strainer back into the saucepan and place on the stovetop over medium-low heat.

4. Using a hand whisk, mix for 5 minutes until thickened, occasionally using a rubber spatula to scrape the sides and base of the pan. Then cook for a couple more minutes, pausing every so often to check if it is bubbling. Once it starts to bubble, pour the mixture into a plastic container. Place plastic wrap directly on top of the pastry cream so that a skin doesn't form; set aside in the refrigerator.

NOTES

- Let the crepes cool down before piping on the cream, or the cream will melt.
- When the pastry cream is thickened over heat, it is easy to burn, so be sure to whisk constantly!
- When the pastry cream is cooling in the fridge, it will thicken even more and become spreadable with a spoon or knife.
- Do not over-whisk the cream, or it will become grainy.
- Cook the crepes as thin as possible for best results.

Vanilla
ICE COFFEE FLOAT

Float drinks are extremely popular throughout Japan, and the Ghibli Park is no exception. There are many options, from cola to melon soda, but one that you really must try is a coffee float! For this version, I recommend a dark-roast coffee to complement the sweet and creamy ice cream—perfect for an indulgent caffeine kick or as a refreshing summer drink.

Serves: 2 | Prep time: 5 minutes |
Cook time: 5 minutes for pour over, 12 hours for cold brew

INGREDIENTS

Pour-Over Method
24 grams (about 4 tablespoons) ground coffee beans, medium to fine-ground
180 ml (¾ cup) hot water
ice cubes

Cold-Brew Method
50 grams (about 3½ ounces) ground coffee beans, medium to coarse-ground
about 2 cups (500 ml) unfiltered water

Add-Ons
vanilla ice cream
gum syrup (optional)
2 mint springs (optional)

POUR-OVER METHOD

1. Add 8 large ice cubes to a glass coffee server. Place your coffee dripper on top and insert a paper coffee filter. Add the ground coffee and gently shake until the top is level. Then place everything on the scale, set it to grams, and make sure it's set at 0.

2. Start your timer and slowly pour in ¼ cup (60 grams) hot water through the coffee filter in clockwise circles. When the timer reaches 45 seconds, pour in 2 more tablespoons hot water (30 grams) and wait another 30 seconds. Repeat three more times. By then the weight on the scale should read 180 grams.

3. Once all the coffee has filtered through, remove the coffee dripper. Swirl the server to melt the ice. If the coffee is still warm, add more ice cubes.

EQUIPMENT

electronic kitchen scale

pour-over coffee dripper

4. Fill two glasses with ice, pour in the coffee, and top each with a scoop of vanilla ice cream and, if desired, a sprig of mint.

COLD-BREW METHOD

1. Pour the coffee grounds into a large jug.

2. Add the water and mix with a large spoon, then cover and refrigerate for 10 to 12 hours.

3. Set a coffee filter and paper over a separate empty jug.

4. Take the cold brew out from the refrigerator and stir one more time. Slowly pour it through the paper filter, so the coffee grounds are filtered out. Do this in batches, as the coffee paper will fill up with the coffee grounds and become harder to filter. Taste and add more cold water until the desired strength is reached.

5. Fill two glasses with ice, pour in the coffee, and top each with a scoop of vanilla ice cream and, if desired, a sprig of mint. If you want the coffee to have a sweeter kick, add a teaspoon of gum syrup.

NOTES

- If you want to stock up on coffee for the weekend, make cold brew in advance. It can be stored in the refrigerator for up to seven days, making it a great option when you're craving a coffee float—not to mention that it's easy to make!

- The cold-brew version has a slightly more mellow flavor than pour-over coffee, with more chocolate and caramel tones. You can also easily adjust the strength by adding more water after brewing.

Summer Festival Shaved Ice
(KAKIGŌRI)

When it's hot out—really hot—and you need to cool down but also want something sweet to reenergize yourself between attractions, this shaved-ice dessert, called kakigōri in Japan, is your answer! A simple dish that never fails to please on a hot day, shaved ice is topped with condensed milk and your favorite fruits. Several topping options are included here. This treat is customizable, delicious, and so addictive that you'll likely be making it on every hot summer day!

Serves: 2 | Prep time: 20 minutes | Cook time: 1 minute

INGREDIENTS
Kakigōri Base
1 cup whole milk

¼ cup sweetened condensed milk

20 ice cubes

Mango Topping
10½ ounces fresh mango, divided

1 tablespoon honey

¼ lemon

KAKIGŌRI BASE
1. Mix the whole milk and condensed milk in a small bowl.

2. Shave the ice into your serving bowl. You can shave the ice using a special ice shaver. If you do not have an ice shaver, you can use a food processor with a grater.

3. Add the milk mixture on top to your liking.

4. Finally, add your preferred topping—options follow.

MANGO TOPPING
1. Cut the 3½ ounces of mango into bite-size pieces and set aside to top the kakigōri.

2. Roughly chop the remaining 7 ounces of mango and add to a blender along with the honey and lemon juice. Blend on high until smooth to create a thin purée. If it seems a little thick, add a splash of water until your preferred consistency is reached.

Strawberry Topping

1 pound and 2 ounces fresh strawberries, divided

¼ cup sugar

¼ cup water

lemon juice, to taste

Matcha Topping

3 tablespoons matcha powder (green tea powder)

¼ cup sugar

¼ cup hot water

1 tablespoon sweetened red bean paste (page 23)

3 shiratama dango (page 24)

matcha (green tea) ice cream

SPECIAL EQUIPMENT

ice shaver or food processor with a grater

STRAWBERRY TOPPING

1. Cut 2 ounces of strawberries into bite-size pieces and set aside.

2. Cut 1 pound of strawberries in half and add to a medium saucepan along with the ¼ cup sugar and 2 tablespoons water.

3. Place on medium-low heat for 10 to 15 minutes, stirring occasionally. The sugar will help break down the strawberries and make them jamlike.

4. Add a squeeze of lemon, and add more water if it is too thick. Remember, as the jam cools in the fridge, it will become slightly lower in viscosity.

MATCHA TOPPING

1. To make the matcha syrup, place the matcha powder, sugar, and hot water in a small bowl and mix to fully incorporate everything. Cover and place in the refrigerator to cool.

2. Place the matcha syrup, red bean, shiratama dango, and matcha ice cream on top of your kakigōri!

NOTES

- Setting your kakigōri serving bowl in the freezer 1 hour ahead of time will help keep it frozen when it's time to enjoy it.

- If you make batches of each topping, you can store them in the fridge and eat them whenever you want!

- It is common for shiratama dango to be used in matcha kakigōri. However, if you cannot find it in your local supermarket, it's fine to skip it!

Iced
MATCHA LATTE

The art and ritual of making matcha have been practiced for centuries in Japan and have become admired worldwide. Earthy and subtly sweet matcha—made from green tea leaves—makes a perfect morning pick-me-up or a cool midday treat during a summertime visit to Ghibli Park.

Serves: 2 | Prep time: 5 minutes | Cook time: 1 minute

INGREDIENTS

¼ teaspoon superfine sugar

¼ cup hot water

2 teaspoons matcha powder

3 tablespoons filtered hot water (175°F)

ice cubes

1½ cups cold whole milk

NOTES

🍃 Matcha is prepared using 175°F water to bring out its natural sweetness. Do not use boiling-hot water—it will spoil the flavor. For a more mellow flavor, use 160°F water.

1. Start by making the syrup. Stir the sugar and ¼ cup water together in a small saucepan over low heat. When the sugar has dissolved, transfer the mixture to an airtight container and refrigerate.

2. Place the matcha powder in the stoneware or glass bowl. Add the 3 tablespoons of filtered hot water and mix vigorously with a chasen whisk, regular whisk, or fork, drawing the letter M as you whisk. This will reduce the bitterness and increase the sweetness.

3. Once a layer of foam has formed on top, lift the whisk to just below the surface and gently break a few of the bubbles.

4. Fill two large glasses with ice and the milk. Stir in the matcha and the chilled syrup to your liking.

No-Fuss
BANANA BREAD

Banana bread is one of those foods that's perfect for any occasion, such as visiting your favorite anime-themed park! This will become your go-to recipe whether you want a comforting pick-me-up or need a dessert for a party.

Serves: 10 | Prep time: 15 minutes | Cook time: 50 minutes

INGREDIENTS
2 cups cake flour

1 teaspoon baking soda

1 tablespoon ground cinnamon

1 teaspoon kosher salt

½ cup (1 stick) unsalted butter, at room temperature

¾ cup brown sugar

1 tablespoon plain Greek yogurt

1 teaspoon vanilla extract

2 large eggs, at room temperature

4 large, overripe bananas

½ cup heavy cream

¼ cup confectioner's sugar

½ teaspoon vanilla extract

1. Preheat the oven to 350°F and line a 9 x 5-inch pan with parchment paper.

2. Sift the cake flour, baking soda, cinnamon, and salt into a medium bowl.

3. In a separate large bowl, add the softened butter and the brown sugar. With a hand mixer, whisk until light and fluffy.

4. Then mix in the yogurt, vanilla, and eggs, one at a time.

5. Mash the bananas in a medium bowl using a fork, leaving a few small whole chunks to create a more interesting texture. Use a rubber spatula to fold the bananas into the butter mixture.

6. Fold in the cake flour mix with a rubber spatula.

7. Pour the batter into the loaf pan and bake on the lowest oven rack at 350°F for approximately 40 minutes, or until cooked through. To test, poke a toothpick into the middle of the loaf; if it comes out dry, then the banana bread is done.

8. Remove the pan from the oven and transfer it to a cooling rack. Let cool for 20 minutes. In the meantime, use a hand mixer or whisk to mix together the heavy cream, confectioner's sugar, and vanilla until medium peaks form.

9. Remove the banana bread from the pan and cut it into 1-inch slices. Serve with the whipped cream.

NOTES

- Make sure to use overripe bananas, as they will be sweeter and soft enough to incorporate into the cake mix.

- If you want to make the banana bread even more indulgent, add some chocolate chips into the mix!

- Take your time making the cake mix to ensure that everything is incorporated. Between each step, use a rubber spatula to scrape the sides and bottom of the bowl to ensure that everything is thoroughly mixed together.

- Want an extra banana kick? Lay slices of raw banana on top of the mix before baking!

Seasonal
FRUIT FOCACCIA

Use a variety of seasonal fruits throughout the year on this scrumptious focaccia—definitely an incentive to visit the park year-round. No matter which fruits you pair with the luxurious pastry cream, you'll have your own personalized Transcontinental Fight Café–inspired dessert to satisfy all your cravings.

Serves: 4 | Prep time: 30 minutes | Cook time: 2 minutes

INGREDIENTS
Pastry Cream (page 126)

24 slices of fruits of choice (see notes and suggestions below)

4 (1-inch) slices of baked focaccia (page 13)

4 teaspoons extra-virgin olive oil

flaky sea salt

Spring Fruits: rhubarb, strawberries

Summer Fruits: raspberries, strawberries, blueberries, cherries, apricots

Autumn Fruits: apples, pears, blackberries, oranges

Winter Fruits: apples, pears, figs

1. Make the pastry cream (see page 126).

2. Spread a layer of the cooled pastry cream on top of the focaccia add and top with your cut fruits. Sprinkle a small amount of sea salt on the fruit to intensify its sweetness. Also add a splash of high-quality extra-virgin olive oil using a spoon and flaky sea salt.

NOTES
- This recipe suggests some classic seasonal fruits from throughout the year, but you can use any kind of fruit that you like. Mix and match, but above all, have fun!
- You can also add fruits on top of the focaccia dough before it is baked. This works brilliantly with fruits such as berries, adding an intense sweetness.

Caramelized-Apple
FOCACCIA

Another dreamy concoction from the Transcontinental Flight Café, this dessert features sweet and sticky cinnamon-spiced apple slices arranged on a luscious pastry cream atop an irresistible piece of focaccia. It doesn't get much better than that, right?

Serves: 4 | Prep time: 40 minutes | Cook time: 20 minutes

INGREDIENTS

Pastry Cream (page 126)

4 (1-inch) slices of baked focaccia (page 13)

3 apples (tart are best, such as Granny Smith)

1 cup granulated sugar

¼ cup of unsalted butter

pinch of kosher salt

1 teaspoon ground cinnamon

1 teaspoon ground nutmeg

½ cup apple juice or water, at room-temperature

4 teaspoons extra-virgin olive oil

1. Make the pastry cream (see page 126).

2. Peel, core, and slice the apples into eighths.

3. Put the sugar in a wide pan over medium to low heat and spread evenly. Wait for it to caramelize, occasionally stirring. When the sugar turns a deep, dark brown color, immediately remove it from the heat. Mix in the unsalted butter until well combined.

4. Add the apples, cinnamon, nutmeg, and salt, mixing to combine everything. Then place on the stovetop over low heat. Add some of the room-temperature apple juice (or water) to loosen, then let bubble away until the apples are cooked through. If the mixture seems a little thick, add more juice. The end consistency should be saucelike and sticky, fully coating the apples.

5. Spread the pastry cream on top of the focaccia using a knife. Then top with the caramelized apples. Drizzle on some of the caramel sauce from the pan using a spoon and 1 teaspoon of extra virgin olive oil.

NOTES

🌸 Depending on your personal preference, you can omit the cinnamon and nutmeg or add more!

🌸 When making the caramel, avoid all contact as it will be very hot and will burn you if it touches your skin. Never add ice-cold apple juice or water to the caramel mix, as it will bubble and spit, potentially causing injuries.

Seasonal
STRAWBERRY PARFAIT

Who doesn't love a parfait? Indulge in this sweet, creamy, and fruity strawberry parfait, perfect for all those sweet tooths out there. And remember, the ingredient proportions are just guidelines. Feel free to adjust them to your liking—and get creative with your parfait design!

Serves: 2 | Prep time: 1 hour | Cook time: 10 minutes

INGREDIENTS
Pastry Cream (page 126)

Strawberry Jam
1 pound strawberries

juice and zest of ½ lemon

½ cup granulated sugar

Parfait
½ cup heavy cream

2 tablespoons granulated sugar

10 to 15 strawberries

3 tablespoons strawberry jam (above)

3 tablespoons granola or cornflakes

1 scoop vanilla ice cream

mint sprigs

1. Make the pastry cream (see page 126).

STRAWBERRY JAM

1. Cut off the green tops and roughly cut the strawberries into quarters.

2. Place the strawberries, the lemon juice, and the ½ cup sugar in a saucepan over medium heat. The strawberries will start to release their water, and the sugar will dissolve.

3. Allow the mixture to bubble gently for approximately 10 minutes, stirring occasionally, until it is jamlike in texture. Add the lemon zest, and the jam is finished!

4. Allow to cool, then place in a sterilized jar, seal, and store in the refrigerator.

PARFAIT

1. Using a hand mixer, combine the cream and sugar until stiff.

2. Cut a few of the strawberries into small cubes, some in thin slices, and some in half.

3. In 2 parfait glasses, layer strawberry jam, granola, and some of the whipped cream. On top of the cream, line the glasses with thin strawberry slices and add some of the diced strawberries in the middle. Add a small amount of strawberry jam and granola, then more whipped cream on top. Repeat one more time, but spoon in the vanilla ice cream before adding the final whipped cream.

4. Arrange thick strawberry slices in a circular shape on top to make a flower pattern. Dot on some of the jam, whipped cream, and granola, and finish with mint sprigs.

Matcha-Lover
PARFAIT

The matcha parfait is very popular in Japan, combining the bitterness of matcha with the sweetness of vanilla ice cream and crunchy granola. It's the perfect dessert to end your long day of adventuring through Ghibli Park.

Serves: 4 | Prep time: 1 hour plus setting time | Cook time: 5 minutes

INGREDIENTS

8 tablespoons granola

¼ matcha chiffon cake (page 166)

12 shiratama dango (page 24)

8 tablespoons sweetened red bean paste (page 23)

Matcha Jelly
2 tablespoons room-temperature water

1 teaspoon gelatin powder

3 tablespoons sugar

1 tablespoon matcha powder

¼ cup water

Milk Jelly
2 tablespoons room-temperature water

1 teaspoon gelatin powder

2 teaspoons sugar

½ cup whole milk

3 tablespoons condensed milk

MATCHA JELLY

1. Start by blooming the gelatin. Add 2 tablespoons of room-temperature water to a small bowl and sprinkle in the gelatin. Stir with a spoon and let sit for a couple of minutes.

2. Meanwhile, add ¼ cup of water to a small saucepan. Sift in the matcha powder. Place on medium-low heat and mix together. Add in the bloomed gelatin and sugar, and mix until everything has dissolved.

3. Place 3 tablespoons of the matcha jelly mix into the parfait glass and put in the fridge to set.

MILK JELLY

1. Start by blooming the gelatin. Add 2 tablespoons of room temperature water to a bowl and sprinkle in the gelatin. Let sit for a couple of minutes.

2. In a saucepan combine the ½ cup milk and 3 tablespoons condensed milk; set on the stovetop over medium-low heat.

Matcha Cream
1¼ cups heavy cream, divided

5 teaspoons matcha powder

¼ cup sugar

3. Add the bloomed gelatin and 2 teaspoons sugar, and mix until everything has dissolved. Remove the pan from the heat and allow to cool slightly.

4. Pour 1½ tablespoons of the milk jelly into the each parfait glass on top of the matcha jelly. Place in the refrigerator to set.

MATCHA CREAM

1. Add ¼ cup of cream to a medium bowl, sift in 5 teaspoons matcha powder, and whisk until well combined.

2. Add the remaining 1 cup of cream and the ¼ cup of sugar. Using a hand mixer, beat until thickened and stiff peaks have formed.

ASSEMBLY

1. Your parfait glasses should already contain the set matcha and milky jelly. Now add to each glass 2 tablespoons red bean paste and a couple of shirat-ama dango to your liking.

2. Add a few pieces of matcha chiffon and 2 tablespoons of granola. Top with the matcha cream and dust with more matcha powder. Use your longest spoons and tuck in!

NOTES

- Depending on the gelatin you are using, the amount may differ from the recipe. Check the instructions on the packet for appropriate ratios. Alternatively, you can substitute agar powder or gelatin leaf.

Summer Fruit Jelly (ANMITSU)

Anmitsu, a classic dessert enjoyed during Japan's long and hot summer, consists of an array of fresh and canned fruits, cubes of jelly, and a luscious scoop of matcha ice cream!

Serves: 4 | Prep time: 15 minutes plus setting time | Cook time: 5 minutes

INGREDIENTS

Gyūhi (type of mochi)
½ cup shirotama flour

½ cup water

½ cup superfine sugar

pink and green food coloring

potato starch, for dusting

Kuromitsu (Black Sugar Syrup)
½ cup brown sugar

¼ cup corn syrup

½ cup water

Fruits (see note on page 152):
8 strawberries

1 orange

4 cherries

1 kiwi

12 slices of fresh or canned yellow peaches

kanten, cut into ½ inch cubes (page 22)

12 shiratama dango (page 24)

GYŪHI

1. In a small bowl, use your hands, or rubber spatula, to mix the shirotama flour with 2 tablespoons water. A dough should start to form. Once it comes together, mix in another 2 tablespoons water. It should start to become a lot looser in consistency.

2. Add the superfine sugar and mix together. Place in a 500-watt microwave oven for 2 minutes. Mix again and then place back in the microwave for another 2 minutes. Repeat this two more times; the mixture should be smooth and get thicker each time.

3. Transfer half the mixture into another small bowl. Add pink food coloring to one bowl and green to the other (or keep the second bowl white). Mix until well combined.

4. Dust the insides of your small containers with potato starch, then transfer the mixture into the containers. Dust the tops with more potato starch and chill in the refrigerator for 1 to 2 hours.

4 tablespoons sweetened red bean paste (page 23)

4 scoops matcha ice cream

SPECIAL EQUIPMENT

2 small rectangular plastic containers for setting gyūhi

5. Remove from the refrigerator and take the gyūhi out of the containers, discarding the excess potato starch. Cut into bite-size pieces. If the texture seems a little hard, let set at room temperature for 5 minutes before cutting.

KUROMITSU

1. Combine the brown sugar, corn syrup, and ½ cup water in a medium saucepan and bring to a boil over medium heat. Mix thoroughly so that everything melts.

2. Once boiling, turn the heat to low heat remove any foam. Then take the pan off the heat and set aside. This will be poured on top at the end. You can store kuromitsu at room temperature in a sterilized and sealed jar.

ASSEMBLY

1. Remove the kanten from its mold and cut it into ½-inch cubes.

2. If you are using fresh fruit, cut it into bite-size pieces.

3. Add the kanten to your serving bowls and top it with a two pieces of gyūhi, 3 pieces of shirotama dango, 2 to 3 slices each of your favorite fruit, 1 tablespoon of sweet red bean paste, and a scoop of matcha ice cream. Drizzle on the kuromitsu!

NOTES

🍄 Often, canned fruits such as yellow peaches and cherries are used in anmitsu. But fresh fruits work just as well! There are no strict rules, so pick your favorite fruits.

🍄 Gyūhi is a type of sweetened mochi that is slightly softer and more delicate. It is traditionally served with anmitsu but it can be skipped if necessary.

Mochi Red Bean Soup (ZENZAI)

Known as zenzai in Japan, this traditional winter dessert is warm, comforting, and deliciously sweet.

Serves: 4 to 6 | Prep time: 5 minutes | Cook time: 1 hour

INGREDIENTS

1 cup raw red (azuki) beans

¾ cup sugar, or as needed

½ teaspoon kosher salt, or as needed

mochi or shiratama dango (page 24)

1. Add the red beans to a medium saucepan of water and bring to a boil over medium-high heat. Once boiling, remove from the heat and strain the beans through a strainer, discarding the water.

2. Return the beans to the saucepan, fill with just enough water to cover, and bring to a boil again over high heat. Once boiling, lower the heat to medium and leave to bubble away, removing any foam that appears using a ladle. If the water falls below the top of the beans, add enough water to cover them.

3. The cooking of the beans is really important in order to get the right texture. To check, pick one up with a rubber spatula and press it between your thumb and index finger. If you can easily break it without using any force, it's ready. In total, this process should take from around 40 minutes.

4. Add the sugar and salt and mix in thoroughly. Turn off the heat and check the consistency. If you would like it a bit more souplike, add more water, turn the heat back on, and bring it back to a boil. Taste the beans and add more sugar and salt if needed. If you want it thicker, use

a ladle to remove some of the water. There is no right or wrong here, it's all up to your preference!

5. If you have premade mochi, place it on a rack in the oven and broil until toasted. If you can't find mochi, use the shirotama dango recipe (page 24).

6. Fill serving bowls with the sweetened red beans, add mochi or shirotama dango balls, and enjoy your sweet dessert!

NOTES

🌸 Zenzai desserts differ in sweetness, so keep tasting and add sugar and salt to your liking.

Crusty Roll with
FRUIT-AND-CREAM FILLING

Fruit-and-cream sandwiches are a quintessential dessert in Japan, often using shokupan (Japanese milk bread), a fluffy, soft white bread. This recipe adds a twist to the Ghibli Park version by using a baguette that's crunchy on the outside and fluffy on the inside.

Serves: 4 to 6 people | Prep time: 10 minutes | Cook time: 5 minutes

INGREDIENTS

1 cup heavy whipping cream

2 tablespoons confectioner's sugar

2-inch vanilla pod or ½ teaspoon vanilla extract

seasonal fruits (see note on page 158)

2 French-style baguettes

Chocolate and Banana Version

pinch of salt

¼ cup 70% dark chocolate

1 tablespoon unsalted butter

2 tablespoons heavy cream

1 banana, sliced in ½-inch pieces

confectioner's sugar, for dusting

SPECIAL EQUIPMENT

piping bag and tip

1. Start by making the whipped cream. Add the cream, the 2 tablespoons confectioner's sugar, and the vanilla to a mixing bowl. If using a vanilla pod, cut it in half and use the back of your knife to scrape the seeds into the bowl.

2. Beat with a hand mixer on medium speed until medium peaks form. If you over-beat your cream, use a rubber spatula to mix in a bit more cold cream, then beat just until medium peaks form.

3. Slice your chosen fruits in half or bite-size pieces.

4. Slice off the ends of the baguette. Cut the baguette in half and hollow out using a using a long, serrated knife or a regular table knife. If the baguette is too long to manage, you can cut into thirds or quarters instead.

5. Insert a piece of fruit at one end of the baguette. Pipe in some whipped cream and then then push in another piece of fruit. Repeat until the inside is full. Slice into 1-inch pieces to serve.

CHOCOLATE AND BANANA VERSION

1. Add water to a small saucepan on the stovetop to fill it a quarter of the way up the sides. Set a mixing bowl on top, large enough that the bottom doesn't touch the water. Add the chocolate to the mixing bowl along with a pinch of salt and the 1 tablespoon butter. Bring the water to a light simmer over medium-low heat to warm up the mixing bowl and melt the chocolate. Mix occasionally with a rubber spatula until fully melted, then remove the bowl from the stovetop and add the 2 tablespoons cream. Stir together and set aside to cool.

2. Cut the baguette in half and hollow out using a using a long, serrated knife or a regular table knife. If the baguette is too long to manage, you can cut into thirds or quarters instead.

3. Using a knife, spread the cooled chocolate inside the baguette.

4. Place a piece of banana at one end of the baguette. Pipe in some whipped cream and then add another piece of banana, pushing the first piece farther into the loaf. Repeat until the inside is full. Dust the top with confectioner's sugar. For extra indulgence, dip the baguette into more chocolate sauce with each bite!

NOTES

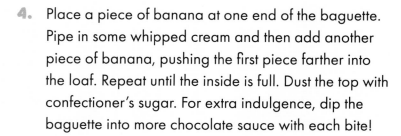

🍄 Popular fruits for this dessert include strawberries, grapes, and kiwis. But there are no rules, so feel free to mix and match to your own liking!

🍄 If you find that hollowing the baguette is too difficult, simply cut it in half from the side, lengthwise and assemble it like a regular sandwich.

Fish Bowl
FRUIT PUNCH

There's no better way to kick off summer than with a fish bowl fruit punch. This recipe makes use of a classic Japanese summer drink, ramune. Popping the marble in the distinctive bottle design and tucking into the refreshingly fizzy and sweet drink cannot be topped! You can even add vanilla ice cream to create the perfect summertime float.

Serves: 2 | Prep time: 5 minutes

INGREDIENTS

10 (½-inch) cubes of kanten (page 22), prepared ahead

4 fresh strawberries

¼ small mango

10 fresh blueberries

2 thin slices lemon

2 bottles original ramune (see note below)

2 fresh or canned cherries

2 mint sprigs

vanilla ice cream (optional)

1. Slice the strawberries in half and cut the mango into small cubes.

2. Remove the kanten from the pan and cut it into pieces similar in size to the mango cubes.

3. Divide all the fruit and the kanten between two serving bowls or tall glasses. Gently stir with a long spoon or mixer, add the lemon slices and then the ramune. Top each serving with a cherry and a sprig of mint.

4. Add a scoop of vanilla ice cream, if you wish, to create a fruit bowl punch float!

NOTES

🍄 Ramune is a classic Japanese soda synonymous with summer and festivals. You can find it in most Asian supermarkets. If not, you can use lemonade or club soda instead.

Perfect
DINNER PARTY CANNOLIS

These cannolis are the perfect dinner-party pleaser. Crispy tube-shaped pastry shells are filled with a zesty ricotta mix and dipped in chocolate and pistachios, making a dessert so addictively delicious that everyone will be asking for the recipe!

Makes: 24 to 28 cannolis | Prep time: 35 minutes plus resting time | Cook time: 20 minutes

INGREDIENTS

Ricotta Filling

32 ounces whole-milk ricotta

1 cup confectioner's sugar

1 tablespoon vanilla extract

1 teaspoon ground cinnamon

juice and zest of 1 lemon

juice and zest of ½ large orange

pinch of kosher salt

RICOTTA FILLING

1. Place the ricotta in a strainer over a glass bowl so the excess moisture can drip down. Cover the top with cheesecloth or plastic wrap and refrigerate overnight.

2. Remove the ricotta from the refrigerator, discard the water in the bowl, and wipe the bowl clean. Then use a rubber spatula to press the ricotta through the strainer into the bowl. This will help make the filling extra smooth.

3. Add the confectioner's sugar, vanilla, cinnamon, lemon juice and zest, orange juice and zest, and a pinch of kosher salt. Using a hand whisk, mix just enough to combine all the ingredients; do not overwhip, or more moisture will be released from the ricotta.

4. Transfer the mixture into a piping bag and set it in the refrigerator to rest.

Canolli Shells

2 cups all-purpose flour

3 tablespoons granulated sugar

½ teaspoon cocoa powder

½ teaspoon instant espresso powder

½ teaspoon kosher salt

3 tablespoons cold lard or unsalted butter, cut into small cubes

2 large egg yolks, plus the whites for brushing the dough

½ cup Marsala wine (see note on page 165)

vegetable oil for frying

1 cup chocolate chips

½ cup crushed pistachio nuts

confectioner's sugar, for dusting

SPECIAL EQUIPMENT

4-inch circular cutter

cannoli forms

piping bag and tip

cooking thermometer

CANNOLI SHELLS

1. In a food processor, mix together the flour, sugar, cocoa powder, espresso powder, and salt. Add the cubed lard or butter and pulse until the mixture is crumbly. Add the 2 egg yolks and the Marsala wine and mix until a wet dough starts to form.

2. Dust a work surface with flour. Transfer the dough to the work surface and knead until smooth, 5 to 10 minutes. Once smooth, form the dough into a ball and cover with plastic wrap. Place in the refrigerator to rest for 2 hours.

3. Fill a large pot half full of vegetable oil and heat to 350°F. Dust a flat work surface with flour and roll your chilled dough into a long rectangle about ⅛-inch thick. Using a 4-inch circular cutter, cut the dough into circles.

4. Place a cannoli mold across the center of one of the circular dough pieces. Wrap each side of the dough around the mold and brush on a little egg white where the dough overlaps. Gently press down so it sticks together. This is important to keep the shells from opening up when deep-fried. Do not wrap the dough tightly around the mold, as it will shrink when deep-fried and would be difficult to take off the mold, or even break.

5. Deep-fry the cannoli shells in batches in the heated oil, molds still in place, for around 2 minutes or until golden brown and slightly puffed up.

6. Use tongs to remove the cannoli shells from the oil and transfer them to a wire rack. Let each shell cool for 30 seconds as you hold the edge of the cannoli form in place with the tongs. Then hold a paper towel in your

other hand and pull the cannoli shell off the tube. Allow to cool on the rack.

ASSEMBLING

1. Place the crushed pistachios and the chocolate chips in separate bowls.

2. When the cannoli shells have cooled, pipe ricotta filling into each shell to fill.

3. Dip half of the cannolis (both ends) into the crushed pistachios each end and the other half into the chocolate chips. Dust the top with confectioner's sugar—and try not to eat them all at once!

NOTES

🌸 Sheep's milk ricotta, which has a slightly tangier taste, is traditionally used for these. However, because it is not as readily available, this recipe instead uses full-fat, whole-milk ricotta. Feel free to use either.

🌸 You don't have to use a food processor for the cannoli dough. You can use a whisk to combine all the dry ingredients, then use a fork or a pair of table knives to create a cutting motion when adding the lard.

🌸 If you cannot find Marsala wine, use a dry white wine instead, with a shot of brandy. This will help puff and crisp up the shells when they are deep-fried.

Matcha
CHIFFON CAKE

Who doesn't love matcha? This recipe makes the most deliciously sweet, moist, and fluffy matcha chiffon cake, perfect for parties or other gatherings, or just as a sweet treat for yourself.

Makes: 1 (7-inch) cake | Prep time: 20 minutes | Cook time: 30 minutes

INGREDIENTS

4 medium eggs

4 teaspoons matcha powder

½ cup cake flour

½ teaspoon baking powder

8 tablespoons of granulated sugar, divided

⅓ cup neutral-flavored cooking oil

2 tablespoons whole milk

2 tablespoons water

whipped cream

sweetened red bean paste (page 23)

1. Set the oven temperature to 350°F. Separate the egg yolks and whites into two separate bowls.

2. Sift the matcha powder, cake flour, and baking powder into a medium bowl.

3. Add 2 tablespoons sugar to the egg yolks and stir with a whisk until paler in color and thickened. It's ready when you can draw the number 8 in the mix with the whisk and it doesn't fade away. Add the oil, milk, and water, whisking to combine.

4. Mix in a third of the flour mixture; repeat until all the flour mix is incorporated. Do not overmix, or gluten will develop and the cake will be harder in texture.

5. Using a hand mixer, beat the egg whites until soft peaks form. Add 2 tablespoons of the remaining sugar and beat on medium speed until incorporated. Repeat for the remaining sugar, beating until stiff peaks form. To check, pull your beater up; the meringue peaks should hold up and not fall over.

6. Use a rubber spatula to incorporate a third of the meringue mix into the cake. Gently fold in to fully

combine. Repeat with the rest of the meringue, being careful not to knock any of the air out of the meringue; this will help the cake to rise.

7. Add the oil, milk, and water, beating until everything is mixed together. Then mix in a third of the flour mixture. Repeat until everything is incorporated. Do not overmix or gluten will develop and the cake will become harder in texture.

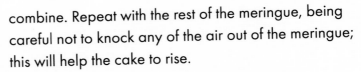

8. Transfer the batter to a chiffon cake pan, tapping it a few times on the countertop to remove any air pockets and ensure that the mixture is evenly spread. Run a wooden skewer through the mix and then tap a few more times on the counter. Then bake for approximately 25 minutes. The cake is ready when a toothpick or wooden skewer inserted in the middle comes out clean.

9. With the cake still in the mold, carefully turn it upside down on a plate. The middle cylindrical part of the cake pan should protrude further than the cake, acting as a stand. Let cool to room temperature. When cooled, run a knife around the edge of the cake to remove it from the mold. Slice and serve with the whipped cream and sweetened red beans.

NOTES

🍄 When whisking the initial egg mix, use a rubber spatula to scrape down the sides and bottom occasionally to make sure everything gets mixed together well.

🍄 The air created in the meringue is the main component that helps the cake rise, so it's important to get this right. Also, fold the meringue into the mix as gently as possible.

Tea-Party
TREATS

This decadent cupcake and cookie combo is perfect for ending your day on a quiet note after a long afternoon wandering the Valley of Witches.

Makes: 14 to 16 cookies and 8 to 10 cupcakes |
Prep time: 1 hour | Cook time: 30 minutes | Cooling time: 1½ hours

INGREDIENTS

Candied Cherries
1 cup fresh cherries, pitted
½ cup granulated sugar
⅙ cup (8 teaspoons) cherry juice
¾ cup water

Jam Cookies
2 cups flour
2 tablespoons cornstarch
pinch of kosher salt
5 ounces (10 tablespoons) unsalted butter, softened
⅔ cup granulated sugar
1 small egg
1 teaspoon vanilla extract
½ teaspoon almond extract
your favorite fruit jelly

CANDIED CHERRIES

1. Combine the cherries, ½ cup sugar, cherry juice, and water in a medium saucepan. Bring to a boil over medium heat, then turn the heat to low so the mixture is just simmering. Leave for approximately 30 minutes, stirring occasionally until the liquid has thickened and reduced.

2. Remove the cherries from the pan and set on parchment paper to cool.

JAM COOKIES

1. Sift the flour, cornstarch, and salt into a medium bowl. Place the softened butter in a separate medium bowl and mix with a hand mixer until slightly paler in color. Add the sugar and mix until light and fluffy. Mix in the egg, vanilla, and almond extract, then add the flour mixture and beat until everything is combined.

2. Transfer the dough to a floured work surface and press into a rectangular shape. Cover with plastic wrap and refrigerate for 1 hour.

Vanilla Icing
½ cup confectioner's sugar

2 to 4 tablespoons whole milk or heavy cream

¼ teaspoon vanilla extract

pinch of salt (optional)

Cupcakes
¾ cup flour

½ teaspoon baking powder

¼ teaspoon baking soda

¼ teaspoon salt

2¼ ounces (4½ tablespoons) unsalted butter, softened

½ cup granulated sugar

2 large eggs, at room temperature

1 teaspoon vegetable oil

1 teaspoon vanilla extract

½ cup whole milk

Cupcake Buttercream
4 ounces (½ cup) unsalted butter, softened

2 cups confectioner's sugar

1 tablespoon vanilla extract

3 tablespoons cream or whole milk

pinch of kosher salt

food coloring (optional)

3. Preheat the oven to 325°F. Remove the dough from the refrigerator and use a rolling pin to roll it to a ⅛-inch thickness. Use a cookie cutter to cut out as many cookies as possible. Reroll the leftover dough and cut more cookies.

4. Place the cookies on a baking tray lined with parchment paper. Bake for around 5 to 8 minutes. You can check if they are done by pressing the edges, which should slightly spring back. Then transfer the cookies to a wire rack and let cool for 30 minutes.

5. In the meantime, make the buttercream by combining the ½ cup confectioner's sugar, 2 to 4 tablespoons milk or heavy cream, and ¼ teaspoon vanilla. If the icing is too stiff, add a little more milk. Add a small pinch of salt for a nice kick! Set aside.

6. Place a small spoonful of your favorite jam in the middle of a cookie, then set another cookie on top and gently press down to spread the jam. Repeat until all the cookies have been used. Spread buttercream on top of the cookies and add a candied cherry to each cookie.

CUPCAKES

1. Preheat the oven to 350°F. Insert liners in the cupcake pan.

2. Sift the flour, baking powder, baking soda, and salt into a medium bowl and mix well.

3. In a separate bowl, using a hand mixer, whisk the softened butter and the 4½ tablespoons sugar until thick, pale, and creamy. Use a rubber spatula to scrape down the sides and bottom occasionally to make sure everything is mixed thoroughly.

4. Mix in one egg at a time, and then vegetable oil and the vanilla extract.

5. Add a third of the flour mix and with a hand whisk, mix until combined. Then add a third of the milk, whisking to combine. Repeat for the remaining flour mix and milk, using a rubber spatula to gently fold everything together. Do not overmix, or the cupcakes will become tough when baked.

6. Scoop the mixture into the cupcake liners, then transfer them to the oven and bake for about 20 minutes. When done, transfer the cupcakes to a wire rack to cool.

7. For the buttercream, place the butter in a large bowl and beat with a hand mixer until pale in color. Slowly add in the confectioner's sugar, beating until the mixture is light and fluffy. Add the milk or cream, vanilla extract, and any desired food coloring and beat until everything is incorporated.

8. Transfer the icing to a piping bag and pipe it on top of the cooled muffins. You can use any piping bag nozzle to make your own design!

RECIPE INDEX

ACKNOWLEDGMENTS

A special thank you goes to Shelona Belfon and the Ulysses Press team for helping and guiding me through the creation of this special cookbook. I would also like to say a huge thank you to my family for supporting me through this process and helping me with all the difficulties.

Next, I would like to express my gratitude to my partner, for whom had she not been around, this book would not have come to be. Thank you for always being there for me, whether it's being a photography assistant, kitchen aide, or moral supporter. Finally, a huge thank you to all my friends and work colleagues who have supported me throughout my career and helped make this book come to life!

ABOUT THE AUTHOR

Andy Cheng, a professional chef turned writer and photographer, has put his passion for cooking to paper as he shares his love of food. His journey started at a young age, learning the basics of cooking from his father. It wasn't until he moved to Japan in 2018 that he delved into the gastronomic world of Japan, studying in kitchens across the country, including a Michelin-starred restaurant nestled in the snowy expanse of Hokkaido. His writing and photography career started to take off as he began writing about Japanese food culture for various web and magazine publishers. Andy now resides in Sapporo, Hokkaido, sharing Japanese food culture and travel with the rest of the world. His debut cookbook, *The Unofficial Ghibli Park Cookbook*, unravels the delectable dishes from Ghibli Park and your favorite Ghibli films, allowing you to re-create the magic in the comfort of your own kitchen. You can follow more of Andy's journey on his Instagram @andychengjp.